Francisco Coronado

and the Seven Cities of Gold

Explorers of New Lands

Francisco Coronado
and the Seven Cities of Gold

Shane Mountjoy

Series Consulting Editor William H. Goetzmann
Jack S. Blanton, Sr. Chair in History and American Studies
University of Texas, Austin

CHELSEA HOUSE
PUBLISHERS
A Haights Cross Communications ◆ Company ®
Philadelphia

COVER: A portrait of Francisco Coronado

CHELSEA HOUSE PUBLISHERS
VP, NEW PRODUCT DEVELOPMENT Sally Cheney
DIRECTOR OF PRODUCTION Kim Shinners
CREATIVE MANAGER Takeshi Takahashi
MANUFACTURING MANAGER Diann Grasse

Staff for FRANCISCO CORONADO
EXECUTIVE EDITOR Lee Marcott
EDITORIAL ASSISTANT Carla Greenberg
PRODUCTION EDITOR Noelle Nardone
PHOTO EDITOR Sarah Bloom
COVER AND INTERIOR DESIGNER Keith Trego
LAYOUT 21st Century Publishing and Communications, Inc.

J-B
CORONADO
350-8630

© 2006 by Chelsea House Publishers,
a subsidiary of Haights Cross Communications.
All rights reserved. Printed and bound in the United States of America.

A Haights Cross Communications ✦ Company ®

www.chelseahouse.com

First Printing

9 8 7 6 5 4 3 2 1

Library of Congress Cataloging-in-Publication Data

Mounjoy, Shane, 1967–
    Francisco Coronado and the seven cities of gold/Shane Mountjoy.
        p. cm.—(Explorers of new lands)
    Includes bibliographical references and index.
    ISBN 0-7910-8631-3 (hardcover)
 1. Coronado, Francisco Vásquez de, 1510–1554—Juvenile literature. 2. Explorers—Spain—
Biography—Juvenile literature. 3. Explorers—America—Biography—Juvenile literature.
4. Cibola, Seven Cities of—Juvenile literature. 5. America—Dscovery and exploration—
Spanish—Juvenile literature. 6. Southwest, New—Discovery and exploration—Juvenile
literature. I. Title. II. Series.
    E125.V3M685 2005
    979'.01'092–dc22
                                                                    2005007518

All links and web addresses were checked and verified to be correct at the time of publication.
Because of the dynamic nature of the web, some addresses and links may have changed since
publication and may no longer be valid.

Table of Contents

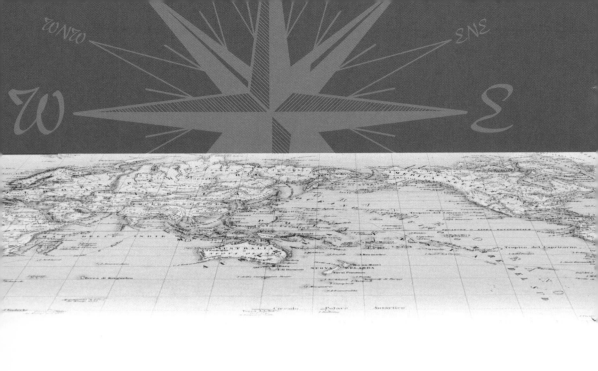

Introduction

by William H. Goetzmann
Jack S. Blanton, Sr. Chair in History and American Studies
University of Texas, Austin

Explorers have always been adventurers. They were, and still are, people of vision and most of all, people of curiosity. The English poet Rudyard Kipling once described the psychology behind the explorer's curiosity:

"Something hidden. Go and find it. Go and
        look behind the Ranges—
Something lost behind the Ranges. Lost and
        waiting for you. Go!" [1]

Miguel de Cervantes, the heroic author of *Don
Quixote*, longed to be an explorer-conquistador. So
he wrote a personal letter to King Phillip II of
Spain asking to be appointed to lead an expedition
to the New World. Phillip II turned down his
request. Later, while in prison, Cervantes gained
revenge. He wrote the immortal story of *Don
Quixote*, a broken-down, half-crazy "Knight of La
Mancha" who "explored" Spain with his faithful
sidekick, Sancho Panza. His was perhaps the first
of a long line of revenge novels—a lampoon of the
real explorer-conquistadors.

Most of these explorer-conquistadors, such as
Columbus and Cortés, are often regarded as heroes
who discovered new worlds and empires. They
were courageous, brave and clever, but most of
them were also cruel to the native peoples they
met. For example, Cortés, with a small band of
500 Spanish conquistadors, wiped out the vast

Aztec Empire. He insulted the Aztecs' gods and tore down their temples. A bit later, far down in South America, Francisco Pizarro and Hernando de Soto did the same to the Inca Empire, which was hidden behind a vast upland desert among Peru's towering mountains. Both tasks seem to be impossible, but these conquistadors not only overcame nature and savage armies, they stole their gold and became rich nobles. More astounding, they converted whole countries and even a continent to Spanish Catholicism. Cathedrals replaced blood-soaked temples, and the people of South and Central America, north to the Mexican border, soon spoke only two languages—Portuguese in Brazil and Spanish in the rest of the countries, even extending through the Southwest United States.

Most of the cathedral building and language changing has been attributed to the vast numbers of Spanish and Portuguese missionaries, but trade with and even enslavement of the natives must have played a great part. Also playing an important part were great missions that were half churches and half farming and ranching communities. They offered protection from enemies and a life of stability for the natives. Clearly vast numbers of natives took to these missions. The missions vied with the cruel native caciques, or rulers, for protection and for a constant food supply. We have to ask ourselves: Did the Spanish conquests raise the natives' standard of living? And did a religion of love appeal more to the natives than ones of sheer terror, where hearts were torn out and bodies were tossed down steep temple stairways as sacrifices that were probably eaten by dogs or other wild beasts? These questions are something to think about as you read the Explorers of New Lands series. They are profound questions even today.

"New Lands" does not only refer to the Western Hemisphere and the Spanish/Portuguese conquests there. Our series should probably begin with the fierce Vikings—Eric the Red, who discovered Greenland in 982, and Leif Ericson, who discovered North America in 1002, followed, probably a year later, by a settler named Bjorni. The Viking sagas (or tales passed down through generations) tell the stories of these men and of Fredis, the first woman discoverer of a New Land. She became a savior of the Viking men when, wielding a broadsword and screaming like a madwoman, she single-handedly routed the native Beothuks who were about to wipe out the earliest Viking settlement in North America that can be identified. The Vikings did not, however, last as long in North America as they did in Greenland and Northern England. The natives of the north were far tougher than the natives of the south and the Caribbean.

Far away, on virtually the other side of the world, traders were making their way east toward China. Persians and Arabs as well as Mongols established a trade route to the Far East via such fabled cities as Samarkand, Bukhara, and Kashgar and across the Hindu Kush and Pamir Mountains to Tibet and beyond. One of our volumes tells the story of Marco Polo, who crossed from Byzantium (later Constantinople) overland along the Silk Road to China and the court of Kublai Khan, the Mongol emperor. This was a crossing over wild deserts and towering mountains, as long as Columbus's Atlantic crossing to the Caribbean. His journey came under less dangerous (no pirates yet) and more comfortable conditions than that of the Polos, Nicolo and Maffeo, who from 1260 to 1269 made their way across these endless wastes while making friends, not enemies, of the fierce Mongols. In 1271, they took along Marco Polo (who was Nicolo's son and Maffeo's nephew). Marco became a great favorite of Kublai Khan and stayed in China till 1292. He even became the ruler of one of Kublai Khan's largest cities, Hangchow.

Before he returned, Marco Polo had learned of many of the Chinese ports, and because of Chinese trade to the west across the Indian Ocean, he knew of East Africa as far as Zanzibar. He also knew of the Spice Islands and Japan. When he returned to his home city of Venice he brought enviable new knowledge with him, about gunpowder, paper and paper money, coal, tea making, and the role of worms that create silk! While captured by Genoese forces, he dictated an account of his amazing adventures, which included vast amounts of new information, not only about China, but about the geography of nearly half of the globe. This is one hallmark of great explorers. How much did they contribute to the world's body of knowledge? These earlier inquisitive explorers were important members of a culture of science that stemmed from world trade and genuine curiosity. For the Polos, crossing over deserts, mountains and very dangerous tribal-dominated countries or regions, theirs was a hard-won knowledge. As you read about Marco Polo's travels, try and count the many new things and descriptions he brought to Mediterranean countries.

Besides the Polos, however, there were many Islamic traders who traveled to China, like Ibn Battuta, who came from Morocco in Northwest Africa. An Italian Jewish rabbi-trader, Jacob d'Ancona, made his way via India in 1270 to the great Chinese trading port of Zaitun, where he spent much of his time. Both of these explorer-travelers left extensive reports of their expeditions, which rivaled those of the Polos but were less known, as are the neglected accounts of Roman Catholic friars who entered China, one of whom became bishop of Zaitun.[2]

In 1453, the Turkish Empire cut off the Silk Road to Asia. But Turkey was thwarted when, in 1497 and 1498, the Portuguese captain Vasco da Gama sailed from Lisbon around the tip of Africa, up to Arab-controlled Mozambique, and across the

Indian Ocean to Calicut on the western coast of India. He faced the hostility of Arab traders who virtually dominated Calicut. He took care of this problem on a second voyage in 1502 with 20 ships to safeguard the interests of colonists brought to India by another Portuguese captain, Pedro Álvares Cabral. Da Gama laid siege to Calicut and destroyed a fleet of 29 warships. He secured Calicut for the Portuguese settlers and opened a spice route to the islands of the Indies that made Portugal and Spain rich. Spices were valued nearly as much as gold since without refrigeration, foods would spoil. The spices disguised this, and also made the food taste good. Virtually every culture in the world has some kind of stew. Almost all of them depend on spices. Can you name some spices that come from the faraway Spice Islands?

Of course most Americans have heard of Christopher Columbus, who in 1492 sailed west across the Atlantic for the Indies and China. Instead, on four voyages, he reached Hispaniola (now Haiti and the Dominican Republic), Cuba and Jamaica. He created a vision of a New World, populated by what he misleadingly called Indians.

Conquistadors like the Italian sailing for Portugal, Amerigo Vespucci, followed Columbus and in 1502 reached South America at what is now Brazil. His landing there explains Brazil's Portuguese language origins as well as how America got its name on Renaissance charts drawn on vellum or dried sheepskin.

Meanwhile, the English heard of a Portuguese discovery of marvelous fishing grounds off Labrador (discovered by the Vikings and rediscovered by a mysterious freelance Portuguese sailor named the "Labrador"). They sent John Cabot in 1497 to locate these fishing grounds. He found them, and Newfoundland and Labrador as well. It marked the British discovery of North America.

In this first series there are strange tales of other explorers of new lands—Juan Ponce de León, who sought riches and possibly a fountain of youth (everlasting life) and died in Florida; Francisco Coronado, whose men discovered the Grand Canyon and at Zuñi established what became the heart of the Spanish Southwest before the creation of Santa Fe; and de Soto, who after helping to conquer the Incas, boldly ravaged what is now the

American South and Southeast. He also found that the Indian Mound Builder cultures, centered in Cahokia across the Mississippi from present-day St. Louis, had no gold and did not welcome him. Garcilaso de la Vega, the last Inca, lived to write de Soto's story, called *The Florida of the Inca*—a revenge story to match that of Cervantes, who like Garcilaso de la Vega ended up in the tiny Spanish town of Burgos. The two writers never met. Why was this—especially since Cervantes was the tax collector? Perhaps this was when he was in prison writing *Don Quixote.*

In 1513 Vasco Núñez de Balboa discovered the Pacific Ocean "from a peak in Darien"[3] and was soon beheaded by a rival conquistador. But perhaps the greatest Pacific feat was Ferdinand Magellan's voyage around the world from 1519 to 1522, which he did not survive.

Magellan was a Portuguese who sailed for Spain down the Atlantic and through the Strait of Magellan—a narrow passage to the Pacific. He journeyed across that ocean to the Philippines, where he was killed in a fight with the natives. As a recent biography put it, he had "sailed over the edge of the world."[4] His men continued west, and the *Victoria*, the last of his five ships, worn and battered, reached Spain.

Sir Francis Drake, a privateer and lifelong enemy of Spain, sailed for Queen Elizabeth of England on a secret mission in 1577 to find a passage across the Americas for England. Though he sailed, as he put it, "along the backside of Nueva Espanola"[5] as far north as Alaska perhaps, he found no such passage. He then sailed west around the world to England. He survived to help defeat the huge Spanish Armada sent by Phillip II to take England in 1588. Alas he could not give up his bad habit of privateering, and died of dysentery off Porto Bello, Panama. Drake did not find what he was looking for "beyond the ranges," but it wasn't his curiosity that killed him. He may have been the greatest explorer of them all!

While reading our series of great explorers, think about the many questions that arise in your reading, which I hope inspires you to great deeds.

Notes

1. Rudyard Kipling, "The Explorer" (1898). See Jon Heurtl, *Rudyard Kipling: Selected Poems* (New York: Barnes & Noble Books, 2004), 7.

2. Jacob D'Ancona, David Shelbourne, translator, *The City of Light: The Hidden Journal of the Man Who Entered China Four Years Before Marco Polo* (New York: Citadel Press, 1997).

3. John Keats, "On First Looking Into Chapman's Homer."

4. Laurence Bergreen, *Over the Edge of the World: Magellan's Terrifying Circumnavigation of the Globe* (New York: William Morrow & Company, 2003).

5. See Richard Hakluyt, *Principal Navigations, Voyages, Traffiques and Discoveries of the English Nation*; section on Sir Francis Drake.

The Seven Cities of Gold

O n the night of July 6, 1540, a group of Spanish explorers was camped a short distance from a small Indian town near the Arizona–New Mexico boundary. Its leader was 30-year-old Francisco Vásquez de Coronado, the governor of a northern province in New Spain (present-day Mexico). Coronado could hardly sleep.

Just over the next hill lay the first of the Seven Cities of Gold: Hawikuh. Finally, he and his men were within reach of the city of Hawikuh.

The Spanish ruler in Mexico, Viceroy Antonio de Mendoza, had spent much of his own money to send Coronado and his men to conquer these cities. Coronado had also spent a lot of his own money for the trip. Before arriving at Hawikuh, the expedition had traveled many miles. The explorers had survived with little food for several weeks. Despite the hardships, they had continued to search, hoping to discover and conquer the Seven Cities of Gold. And on this night, Coronado and his men were very near Hawikuh.

This was not the first time a Spanish expedition had come so close to Hawikuh. The Indians attacked the earlier team and killed many of its men. But that group was not armed. The first expedition was only a scouting party made up of Indians and priests. The leader of that expedition, Friar Marcos, now accompanied Coronado. The Catholic priest had never entered the city, but only saw it from a distance. After the local Indians attacked the advance party, the friar feared for his life. Marcos decided it was better to leave while he still could and make a report to Viceroy Mendoza. But before leaving, the friar climbed a nearby hill and looked at Hawikuh.

The city, said Marcos, was "situated on a level stretch on the brow of a roundish hill. It appears to be a very beautiful city, the best I have seen in these parts. . . . The town is bigger than the city of Mexico. At times I was tempted to go to it, because I knew that I risked nothing but my life, which I had offered to God the day I commenced the journey. Finally I feared to do so, considering my danger and that if I died, I would not be able to give an account of this country, which seems to me to be the greatest and best of discoveries."[1] Marcos claimed that the city was one of the Seven Cities of Gold.

A LEGENDARY TALE

The Seven Cities of Gold! Coronado first heard the story of the celebrated cities when he was a boy in Spain. Indeed, the legend of the Seven Cities of Gold did not come from American Indians. It was a story the Spanish brought with them when they came to the New World. The story dates back a thousand years ago. Around the year 1000, the Christian Spanish were at war with the Spanish Muslims, or Moors. The Moors had conquered much of what is now Spain. The Spanish Christians did not want the Moors to rule over them. According to legend, an archbishop named Oporto decided to escape Moorish control. He and six other bishops, along with their congregations, left Spain to get away from the Muslims. When they left, they took with them a great amount of gold and treasure. They set sail, hoping to reach the Fortunate Isles.[2] Unfortunately, a storm blew them off course. The storms pushed them far out into the Atlantic Ocean.

The seven bishops and their congregations had no choice but to land where the winds took them. According to the legend, they landed on an island called Antilia. There, the bishops burned their ships and set about building seven cities, which became prosperous. Stories about these cities spread, detailing the vast wealth they supposedly contained.

In one of these stories, a Portuguese sailor claimed he once saw the island, where gold was abundant. The traveler claimed that even the sand on Antilia's beach contained gold. Early Spanish

A nineteenth-century picture shows life in a Zuñi pueblo. On July 6, 1540, Francisco Vásquez de Coronado and his men were camped near a similar pueblo—Hawikuh—and hoped they had found one of the fabled Seven Cities of Gold.

explorers often looked for the fabled island, but none ever saw it. Columbus never found the legendary island. Other explorers looked in vain. No real proof existed. But that did not stop

Spanish mapmakers from placing the cities on maps, locating them somewhere north of present-day Florida. The story seemed too good to be true. And yet, many young Spanish boys grew up hoping to find the Seven Cities of Gold.

And now Coronado and his men believed that only a small hill separated them from one of the Seven Cities of Gold. All of the money, the many preparations, the long miles, and the lack of food—everything would be worth it in the morning. Tomorrow great riches surely awaited Coronado and his men. Tomorrow they hoped to walk streets of gold. Tomorrow they hoped to become the first Spaniards to enter the gleaming cities. Tomorrow they hoped to conquer a legend!

Test Your Knowledge

1 Where was the village of Hawikuh located?
a. Near the center of what is today Mexico
b. On what is today the island of Cozumel
c. Near what is today the border between Arizona and New Mexico
d. Near what is today Mexico City

2 Who was Antonio de Mendoza?
a. A priest who led a prior expedition
b. The viceroy of Mexico
c. A rival of Coronado's
d. None of the above

3 What happened to the first expedition to Hawikuh?
a. The unarmed explorers were attacked by Indians.
b. The explorers befriended the Indians and returned with much gold.
c. The armed explorers defeated the Indians and took their gold.
d. The expedition became lost and never got close to Hawikuh.

4 Where did the legend of the Seven Cities of Gold originate?

a. In the New World

b. In Spain

c. In the Bible

d. None of the above

5 Who was the only person to claim to have actually seen the fabled island of Antilia?

a. A Portuguese sailor

b. A Spanish priest

c. An Aztec Indian

d. None of the above

ANSWERS: 1. c; 2. b; 3. a; 4. b; 5. a

The Explorer's
Early Life

AN EXPLORER IS BORN

In 1510, Francisco Vásquez de Coronado was
born in the city of Salamanca. Located in west-
central Spain, the city has a rich history. It is an
ancient city, dating back to pre-Roman times. At one
point in its history, Rome established control in the

9

area. Rome built a bridge there that still spans the Tormes River.

In 220 B.C., Salamanca fell under attack by Hannibal, a general from the North African city of Carthage. Carthage was at war with the mighty Roman Empire at the time. Coronado's home city was within the Roman province of Lusitania. Hannibal passed through Spain before crossing the Alps with war elephants. When he passed through, Hannibal conquered the city.

About 900 years later, the Moors, who conquered much of Spain, also dominated Salamanca. The city changed hands several times before the Christian forces finally won control of the city in the eleventh century.

Salamanca also had a world-famous institution of higher learning. King Alfonso IX founded the University of Salamanca in 1218. It is the oldest university in Spain. The university enjoyed much acclaim. Pope Alexander IV described it as "one of the four leading lights of the world."[3] For many years, the university was the city's primary claim to fame. In the mid-sixteenth century, Francisco Coronado became another leading light for Salamanca.

Coronado was born into nobility. His family name was Vásquez, not Coronado. However, the English (and Americans) did not follow the Spanish naming system, so he is usually known as Coronado. He was the second of four sons. His parents were Juan Vásquez de Coronado and Isabel de Luxán. His father was descended from "the royal blood of France."[4] His parents owned a large estate. It is likely that his parents were important and wealthy enough that they personally knew the king and queen of Spain. Since Francisco had an older brother, however, he did not receive much of an inheritance. The Coronado family kept the Spanish tradition of giving most of the inheritance to the eldest son. Families expected younger sons to make their own fortune. Many younger sons became priests. Others entered into government service at the royal court. Still others became soldiers. Francisco's two sisters became nuns.

Francisco Coronado benefited from the advantages of nobility. He probably attended school. Historians know little about his education, but younger sons in noble families at that time received

It is possible that Francisco Vásquez de Coronado may have pursued his interest in science at the University of Salamanca in Spain, shown here. This university, which was founded in 1218, had a good reputation for scientific studies.

valuable instruction. Coronado learned to read and write. He probably studied science, mathematics, philosophy, and Latin. Later in life, Coronado seemed especially interested in science. Perhaps he even studied at the well-known University of Salamanca, which had a reputation for its study of science.

Since there was an older heir to his family's estate, Francisco and two of his brothers faced a difficult decision. Each could cut back on his lifestyle or each could win his own fortune. Each of the younger three Coronado brothers chose to try his hand at making his own fortune. And each of them managed to make history. One of them, Juan Vásquez, became the first governor of Costa Rica. The youngest brother, Pedro, knew King Phillip II of Spain and "later fought valiantly in the navy of Don Juan of Austria."[5] Each of the younger three brothers entered into government service. And each enjoyed successful careers.

When Francisco Coronado was a teenager, he followed the custom of the day for those younger sons born into nobility: either go to a colony or go to the royal court. Coronado eventually did both. But first, he served at the royal court. At the time,

As a teenager, Francisco Coronado served in the royal court of the king of Spain, Charles I, above. Charles also ruled the Holy Roman Empire, and was known as Charles V since he was not the first emperor with that name.

the king of Spain, Charles I, was the most powerful monarch in the world. (Charles also ruled the Holy Roman Empire. Since he was not the first Holy Roman emperor to have that name, he is also known as Charles V.) It was through his experiences at court that Coronado gained a trustworthy friend and powerful ally. This friend later helped him gain enduring fame. This friend was Antonio de Mendoza.

A POWERFUL FRIEND

Coronado met Antonio de Mendoza while he served at the royal court. A distant relative to King Charles, Mendoza had served Spain as ambassador to Rome. He was one of the king's favorites. Although Mendoza was about 20 years older than Coronado, the two quickly became good friends. Mendoza was more established and helped his young friend. He hired Coronado as his assistant.

Coronado enjoyed some success in the Spanish royal court. But he had little future in Spain. Instead, opportunities in the New World soon presented themselves to Mendoza and his young assistant. Coronado recognized the possibilities for advancement there. He wanted to go to New Spain. Mendoza took him there—and it was there that Coronado lived the rest of his life.

TO MEXICO

In 1530, Charles appointed Antonio de Mendoza as viceroy of New Spain. The viceroy—something like a governor—was the most important royal official in the New World. The viceroy acted on behalf of the king in the colony. For five years, Mendoza was not able to go to New Spain. Finally, he left Europe in 1535. When he went, the new viceroy took his young assistant, 25-year-old Francisco Coronado, with him.

After arriving in Mexico, Coronado soon established himself as a capable worker. One of the most important men in Mexico City had been Alonso de Estrada. Estrada was an illegitimate son of King Ferdinand. This means he was born to Ferdinand and a woman other than his wife, Isabella. Raised in the royal court, he moved his family to New Spain in 1523. There, he served as the royal treasurer of Mexico. Earlier, he had even served as governor of the colony. Estrada died in 1531. When Coronado arrived in 1535, the Estrada family was very wealthy and influential.

Coronado met and married Estrada's daughter, Beatriz, who was a cousin of King Charles's. (Charles was Ferdinand and Isabella's grandson through their daughter Joanna, the half-sister of Alonso de Estrada.) As a result of his marriage into the Estrada family, Coronado gained a large estate. What little is known of Beatriz indicates that she was a kind woman who loved her husband. Coronado and Beatriz had five children. Their first child and only son died as an infant. On his long journey searching for the Seven Cities of Gold, Coronado missed his wife and children.

Coronado enjoyed success in Mexico. Not long after his marriage, in 1537, a rebellion rose up in one of the silver mines near modern-day Taxco, Mexico. A group of black slaves and Indians seized control of the mine. Mendoza ordered Coronado to lead a force to put down the revolt. He did so, with few casualties. This impressed the viceroy. Soon after, Mendoza promoted Coronado, naming him the governor of New Galicia. (Today, the Mexican states of Sinaloa and Nayarit make up what was

New Galicia.) This province was northwest of Mexico City. Coronado and his wife moved to the province's capital, Compostela. He might have remained there, but the appearance of four strangers in Mexico City changed everything for Coronado.

STORIES OF THE GOLDEN CITIES

In 1536, four ragged-looking men walked into Sinaloa, in western Mexico. The men wore dirty and worn-out clothes made of animal "skins and tattered cloth."[6] The men were dirty and hungry. They had long beards. They looked half-starved. Three of them were Spaniards; the fourth was a black slave. Coronado was in Compostela and did not know any of the four men. But the story they told would change Coronado's life. Their story began about nine years before.

The four men were survivors of a failed expedition to Florida. The expedition had begun in 1527. Pánfilo de Narváez led the expedition. Narváez was a Spanish explorer. He tried to establish a colony in Florida. After landing on the Florida coast, Narváez sent the ships back to Mexico. Then he and his men began exploring inland. The expedition of some

300 men searched for gold, without success. The Spaniards were often cruel toward the natives. Some of Narváez's men died from disease. Others were killed in continued fighting with Indians. Lacking food, the men killed their horses in order to eat. Finally, facing starvation, Narváez decided to abandon the failed colony. To leave, the group built crude ships. They set sail from the western coast of Florida, into the Gulf of Mexico. But after leaving Florida, he and his men sailed into severe storms. The storms separated the simple boats. Some boats sank, drowning the men. The storm carried other boats out to sea—they were never heard from again. One boat alone survived. In it were several Spaniards, including the four ragged-looking men. One of them was Alvar Núñez Cabeza de Vaca. He and his men landed on a small island off the coast of Texas, near present-day Galveston.

Friendly natives cared for Cabeza de Vaca and his men. Even with the Indians' help, the Spaniards faced many dangers. Disease and starvation killed many of the Indians and Spaniards. By spring, only 15 of the men from the Narváez expedition survived.

Not all of the Indians thought it was a good idea to help the strangers. Disease and starvation caused some Indians to distrust the Spaniards. The expedition's survivors realized they needed to make themselves useful. At just the right time, Cabeza de Vaca pretended to be a medicine man. He

Viceroy Mendoza: A Model Leader

Antonio de Mendoza was more than just a good friend to Coronado. He was also a talented administrator who set the example for how a Spanish viceroy ought to act. He was most likely the greatest administrator working for Spain in the New World.

Historians credit Mendoza with improving relations with the Indians in Mexico. When he came to Mexico in 1535, he brought the first printing press to the New World. To equip Indians socially and spiritually, Mendoza built schools and churches. To better the economy of New Spain, Mendoza improved farming and industry there.

Under Mendoza, New Spain benefited from stability and a growing economy. Historians mimicked the native medicine men who recited chants and made motions with their hands over sick patients. He did this to protect himself from the Indians. It seemed to work, though Cabeza de Vaca doubted his own healing abilities. For several years, the remaining men struggled to survive. They did

also believe that Mendoza's leadership was the foundation that allowed Spain to rule there until Mexico achieved independence in 1821. Some even call Mendoza "the Good Viceroy" because of his able leadership.*

Other Spanish colonies did not enjoy the peace and stability that Mendoza achieved in Mexico. One of these colonies was Peru, in South America. In 1551, the king of Spain named Mendoza the new viceroy of Peru. Mendoza went south to deal with the problems there. But he was not as successful. He only lived about a year after going to Peru, dying in 1552.

* Steven Otfinoski, *Francisco Coronado: In Search of the Seven Cities of Gold* (New York: Benchmark Books, 2003), 62.

what they needed to do to remain alive. They pretended to be medicine men. They helped the Indians trade. They worked as slaves. All the while, they thought about getting back to New Spain.

After several years, only five of the men were alive. Four of them decided to head south and west to reach New Spain. The fifth man refused to go. The other four left without him. They were Cabeza de Vaca, Andres Dorantes de Carranca, Alonzo del Castillo Maldonado, and a slave named Estevanico (usually known as Esteban). Spanish slave hunters found them in Sinaloa a year later and took them to Mexico City in the summer of 1536. Their arrival changed the future of Francisco Coronado.

Cabeza de Vaca described the lands they had seen. He also talked about great Indian cities to the north. Many Spaniards hoped the cities that Cabeza de Vaca had visited were the Seven Cities of Gold. The men met with Viceroy Mendoza. They told him stories about some grand Indian cities. They had not been to the cities, but they had heard about them.

Viceroy Mendoza eagerly listened. He questioned Cabeza de Vaca closely to learn all he could about the region to the north. Mendoza was convinced that the Seven Cities of Gold did exist. He thought that if the cities really existed, there was a chance to discover and claim them. And if the cities really existed, there was a chance to become very wealthy.

To determine the truth of the stories, Mendoza turned to the young governor of New Galicia to lead an expedition. The viceroy knew Coronado was capable. He knew that he could rely on Coronado. And more important, he trusted Coronado perhaps more than he trusted anyone else in New Spain. Mendoza chose Coronado to head the expedition to find the Seven Cities of Gold. Thirty-year-old Francisco Coronado stood ready to expand the claims of the Spanish Empire. In 1540, he set out to find the Seven Cities of Gold.

Test Your Knowledge

1 Coronado's home city of Salamanca
was once ruled by
a. the Romans.
b. Hannibal.
c. the Moors.
d. all of the above.

2 How did the young Coronado impress
Viceroy Mendoza?
a. By ending piracy in the waters around
Mexico
b. By discovering a profitable silver
mine
c. By efficiently ending a rebellion
by slaves and Indians
d. All of the above

3 How did the survivors of the failed Narváez
expedition win the confidence of the local
Indians?
a. The Spaniards promised the tribal leaders
gold and riches.
b. The Spaniards claimed to be medicine
men.
c. The Spaniards claimed to be messengers
of the gods.
d. None of the above.

4 How did Cabeza de Vaca and his companions get to Mexico City?
   a. They were found by slave hunters, who brought them to the city.
   b. They bribed local Indian guides to take them to the city.
   c. They hiked through jungles and deserts until they stumbled upon the city.
   d. None of the above.

5 For which of the following is Viceroy Antonio de Mendoza known?
   a. Bringing the first African slaves to Mexico
   b. Damaging relations between the Spaniards and local Indians
   c. Bringing the first printing press to the New World
   d. All of the above

ANSWERS: 1. d; 2. c; 3. b; 4. a; 5. c

Coronado's World

SPAIN

To understand the significance of Coronado's journey, it is important to look at Spain and its role in the world in 1540. When Coronado was born in 1510, he was born into a Spain that stood ready to be the world power. Spain is in southwestern Europe, on the Iberian Peninsula. (The name Iberian Peninsula comes from the ancient Greeks, who called those who lived there Iberians. It is probable that those people and the peninsula took their name from the peninsula's second-longest river, the Ebro, or Iberus.) Today, Spain and Portugal occupy the entire peninsula. In 1510, Spain was essentially a united country. The country had endured many years of fighting. The fighting dated back to the 700s, when a group of people invaded the Iberian Peninsula from northern Africa. These attackers were the Moors. The Moors were Arab Muslims who expanded their territory into Europe. They crossed the Mediterranean Sea near Gibraltar and captured most of the Iberian Peninsula by 718. But the Moors never succeeded in driving all of the Christian kingdoms from the Iberian Peninsula. For nearly 400 years, the mountainous region in northern Spain was all that remained free of Moorish control.

It was in southern Spain where the Moors had their center of power. They made the city of Córdoba their capital. Córdoba was on an important river (the Guadalquivir). During Moorish rule, a blending of Spanish and Moorish culture flourished. The Moors made advances in architecture, celebrated the arts, and encouraged the writing and study of literature. The Moors built mosques, which are Muslim places of worship. They also built *alcazars*, or castles. The Moors preserved many ancient Greek and Latin writings, as well as writings from the Middle East. European scholars traveled to Spain to study these ancient works. The Moors allowed Christians and Jews to live in their society. Many of these non-Moorish peoples helped contribute to the flourishing culture.

But even as their culture prospered, the Moorish military grew weaker. The central Moorish government also grew weak. Many of the small, independent Moorish states and cities no longer supported the central government. Although the Moors controlled most of Spain, they allowed some of the Christian kingdoms to continue ruling at the local level. As the central government weakened, these Christian kingdoms grew tired of Moorish rule. Soon, they challenged the Moors for control.

Over time, some of the remaining Christian kingdoms grew stronger. These kingdoms began to

A Moorish painting from 1229 shows the conquest of Mallorca during the fight between the Christians and the Moors in Spain. The Moors, Muslims from North Africa, captured most of the Iberian Peninsula by 718 and were not driven away until 1492.

reclaim parts of Spain. At the start, the Christian kingdoms were only in northern Spain. But they enjoyed success and slowly forced the Moors to southern Spain. Finally, by the late 1200s, the Moors controlled only the southern Kingdom of Granada.

The Moors struggled to keep their independence from the Christian kingdoms. This task
became more difficult as the fighting continued.
The Christian kingdoms grew stronger, and
united into fewer and fewer kingdoms. By 1300,
there were only three kingdoms that controlled
all of the non-Moorish parts of Spain. These were
the Christian kingdoms of Aragon, Castile, and
Navarre. Castile—the largest and most powerful
of the kingdoms—controlled most of Spain.
Aragon ruled most of eastern Spain and the
Balearic Islands in the Mediterranean Sea.
Navarre—the smallest of the Christian kingdoms—
was near the mountains in northern Spain.

In 1469, two of the Spanish kingdoms combined
to grow even stronger. In that year, Ferdinand of
Aragon and Isabella of Castile were married. Their
marriage unified the largest and most powerful Spanish kingdoms. Within ten years, King
Ferdinand and Queen Isabella enjoyed complete
control over their combined territories: Aragon
and Castile. Nearly all of Christian Spain was
now unified and ready to claim the rest of the
Iberian Peninsula from the Moors. As for the small

kingdom of Navarre, Castile conquered it in 1512. This final victory united all of Christian Spain under a single ruler.

After their marriage united most of Spain, Ferdinand and Isabella decided to push the remaining Moors in Granada off the Iberian Peninsula. Under their leadership, the Moors were finally defeated in January 1492. To strengthen their hold, Ferdinand and Isabella also expelled any Jews who refused to convert to Christianity. A fight that began as a way to unify Spain under one kingdom ended up being a war to rid Spain of non-Christians.

SPAIN DISCOVERS THE NEW WORLD

Of course, Spain did more than just defeat the Moors in 1492. That was the year that Christopher Columbus sailed to the New World. Columbus was born in Genoa, Italy, but he sailed for Spain when he discovered the West Indies. It was Portugal, however, not Spain, that first used exploration to build a trade empire. Europeans wanted to trade with the Far East. Asia offered tea, spices, and other goods that Europeans wanted. Long distances separated Asia and Europe. Many rivers and mountain ranges made trade long and difficult. In the early 1400s, Portugal began exploring for ways to travel to and from India and the East Indies. One early Portuguese leader in exploration was Prince Henry the Navigator. He encouraged his countrymen to explore parts of western Africa. These expeditions resulted in trade with African natives. This trade included gold, ivory, and slaves. From this African trade, Portugal became a wealthy nation. Even though Portugal was one of Europe's smallest countries, its explorers later sailed all the way around the southern tip of South Africa.

The Spanish rulers saw how Portugal became wealthy. Under Ferdinand and Isabella, Spain followed Portugal's example and created trading posts and colonies outside of Europe. Spain was just one of the many European countries that wanted to trade with the Far East. Since Portugal controlled African trade, Spain looked elsewhere for colonies.

Christopher Columbus helped Spain find good places for colonies. Columbus, like the Portuguese, wanted to find a trade route to the East Indies. He and most geographers of his day thought that the world was round. Therefore, he decided to sail west to get to the East Indies. But he incorrectly believed that the world was much smaller than it is. So when he sailed west, he failed to reach Asia. Instead, he landed on a group of islands in the Caribbean. Columbus thought he had landed in the East Indies. As a result, he claimed the lands for Spain and called the people he found there "Indians."

A POWERFUL WEAPON: RELIGION

Spanish Christians spent nearly 800 years fighting the Moors. During that time, military drive and religious passion were combined. Political and religious goals became one goal. Religious unity became the same thing as national unity. And the Spanish believed that national unity was accomplished through religious unity. Spain used eagerness and zeal to defeat the Moors. They used the same eagerness and zeal to establish an empire in the Americas. First, they conquered the native peoples. Then, they converted the natives to Christianity. To the Spanish, religious conversion was only possible after gaining political control. And religious conversions helped keep political control. This view came from the Spanish experience in the Moorish wars.

King Ferdinand and Queen Isabella set up the Spanish Inquisition as a court to deal with people who did not follow Roman Catholic teachings. Above, people who refused to convert are burned at the stake. Spain later used the Inquisition against natives in the Americas.

The Spanish often used religion to justify their wars. Since they spent so much time fighting the Spanish Muslims, this made sense. Castile and Aragon based their war for control of Spain on religious differences between themselves and the Islamic Moors. To help in their fight against the Moors in conquered areas, Ferdinand and Isabella set up a special court in 1480 to deal with people who did not follow Roman Catholic teachings. This court was the Spanish Inquisition, which held enormous power. The Inquisition had the power to put people in prison or even put them to death. If individuals did not accept Christianity, they often faced death. Later, Spain used the Inquisition against natives in their American colonies to establish and maintain control.

Another impact of the Moorish wars was that Spain grew more focused on making war. Soon, Spain fought not just the Moors within its own borders, but also a rival European power, France. All of these battles helped produce men who relied on fighting to solve their problems. Many of these men ended up going to the New World. Coronado did not receive training as a soldier, but many of the men he later served with in Mexico were soldiers. And it was a soldier, Hernándo Cortés, who succeeded in capturing Mexico from the Aztecs.

GETTING RICH AND CONVERTING NATIVES

With their homeland secure against non-Christian threats, the Spanish shifted their energies to conquering and converting other people. Within just a few years of Columbus's initial voyage across the Atlantic, it soon became clear that a land of opportunity awaited brave souls. The New World seemed to offer two great opportunities for the Spanish: gold and converts to Christianity. Almost immediately, the Spanish realized the possibility of acquiring gold. Columbus himself had reported on this when he saw the natives wearing gold jewelry "attached to holes in their noses."[7] He could not understand the natives and lacked an interpreter. Through primitive sign language, Columbus learned that the gold had come from the south. They also told him about a ruler in the south who had large amounts of gold— so much gold that he ate and drank from golden plates and cups.[8] A Spanish conquistador named Francisco Pizarro later discovered and conquered this southern ruler: Moctezuma. But there were also stories of gold in the north. These stories usually included descriptions of entire cities made of gold.

But Columbus saw another way for Spain to get rich from the natives in the New World: slavery. He believed that the Indians would make good slaves, observing that the natives were "fit to be ordered about and made to work."[9] Spanish explorers who followed Columbus later placed many American Indians into slavery. And they became rich from doing so.

Besides gold and slavery, Columbus also saw the prospects for Catholic mission work in the New World. He wrote, "I believe they would readily become Christians, for they seem to have no religion."[10] For many Spanish explorers, this report justified conquering the "pagan" peoples in the Americas. Almost all of the early Spanish military expeditions included Catholic priests to convert the local natives.

Columbus hoped to become wealthy by finding gold in the New World. But he never discovered much gold. Instead, his stories inspired young ambitious men from Spain. Rumors of gold, large tracts

(continued on page 40)

Cortés: The Misuse of Religion

Hernándo Cortés conquered the Aztec Empire with about 500 Spanish soldiers. It is true that the Spanish showed bravery and used advanced weaponry as they defeated the huge Indian armies. But Cortés also used religion as a mighty weapon against the Aztecs. After defeating the Aztecs, Cortés sought to convert as many natives as possible. To do this, he brought priests with him on his conquest. As soon as an area fell under his control, the process of conversion began. Priests shared their message with the conquered peoples.

But it was how Cortés used Christianity after seizing control that demonstrates his ruthlessness. The Spanish viewed any Indians who refused to accept Christianity as possible rebels. As a result, such Indians faced mistreatment at the hands of the Spanish. On the other hand, the Europeans warmly accepted Indians who converted.

It is true that Cortés was a "master manipulator of man."* He used religion—his religion—to manipulate those he conquered. And he was not opposed to using unusual methods in converting the Indian masses. Cortés replaced pagan altars with Christian shrines. The natives sang and danced in their pagan rituals, so he used song and dance in Christian celebrations. Once, he realized that the Aztecs viewed the eagle as a sacred bird.

He simply replaced the dove with an eagle to represent the Holy Spirit.**

So why did Cortés—a man of war and bloodshed—show such concern for the spiritual lives of the people he conquered? Why did he take care to teach the Indians Christianity? In part, it was due to the political situation in New Spain. To keep his position, Cortés brandished both the sword and the cross while taking control in Mexico. His passion for evangelism also might have been motivated by his beliefs. He viewed himself as a "devout Catholic."*** It seems strange that war and compassion could be so evident in one person. But Cortés was not unique in this regard. Spanish society seemed to produce this sort of double identity. The mixing of war and religion was so thorough that even the priests who went with Cortés participated in the battles. Cortés and his army brought with them the sword and the cross. They conquered the locals and converted them to Christianity. They brought sixteenth-century Spanish culture to the Americas.

   * Karl E. Meyer, *Teotihuacan*. (New York: Newsweek, 1973), 97.

  ** Winifred Hulbert, *Latin American Backgrounds*. (New York: Friendship Press, 1935), 26.

*** Fernando Benitez, (translated by Joan MacLean) *The Century After Cortés*. (Chicago: The University of Chicago Press, 1962), 147.

(continued from page 37)

of land, and many unconverted Indians drew men to the New World. Many Spanish men listened to the stories of the newly discovered lands. Many dreamed of the possibilities in the New World. Many Spanish men wished to find gold, conquer land, acquire slaves, and convert the natives to Catholicism. And many Spanish men eventually left their homeland to follow their dreams in the New World. One of these men was Francisco Coronado. Both the desire for gold and the focus on religion affected Coronado in Mexico.

Test Your Knowledge

1 What is an *alcazar?*
   a. A type of Spanish sailing ship
   b. A gold coin invented by
      the Moors
   c. A castle built by the Moors
   d. A type of sword

2 Which of the following contributed to
   the decline of Moorish power in Spain?
   a. The weak central government,
      which lacked the support of small
      Moorish states
   b. The growing power of the Christian
      kingdoms of northern Spain
   c. The marriage of Ferdinand of Aragon
      and Isabella of Castile
   d. All of the above

3 Which of the following motivated Spanish
   explorers to travel to the New World?
   a. The search for gold and riches
   b. The desire to increase the territory
      and influence of Spain
   c. The desire to gain converts for the
      Catholic Church
   d. All of the above

4 How was Coronado unlike his countryman,
   Hernándo Cortés?
   a. Coronado had no formal military training.
   b. Coronado was not a Catholic.
   c. Coronado was not interested in gold or
      treasure.
   d. None of the above.

5 How did Hernándo Cortés use his power
   to convert native people in the Americas
   to Catholicism?
   a. He bribed the native people with
      trinkets from Spain.
   b. He replaced native idols with Catholic
      symbols.
   c. He used persuasion but never
      military force.
   d. All of the above.

ANSWERS: 1. c; 2. d; 3. d; 4. a; 5. b

Friar Marcos

THE FRIAR MARCOS SCOUTING PARTY

The Spaniards did not know much about the lands north of Mexico. Viceroy Mendoza sent a large scouting party ahead of Coronado to help locate the Seven Cities of Gold. A Catholic priest, Marcos de Niza, led this group. Most knew the priest as Friar Marcos.

Mendoza ordered Friar Marcos to search out and verify the existence of the Seven Cities. The party also included Esteban, the black slave and one of the four survivors of the Narváez expedition.

This scouting party left Mexico City in the spring of 1539. To help calm the natives, Friar Marcos sent Esteban ahead with a group of Indians. This group entered villages before the monk and his team. Friar Marcos ordered Esteban to give reports on the size and wealth of any cities. This posed a problem, though—the slave was unable to read or write. To overcome this difficulty, the two worked out a signal. Esteban sent crosses as his message: the larger the cross, the richer the country.

The two groups traveled in this manner for some time. On one occasion, Friar Marcos could not believe his eyes. Esteban's messengers carried a wooden cross as large as a man! Still more large crosses followed this first one. The monk could only imagine what great wealth awaited him. The local Indians continued to amaze him with stories of great wealth in the country ahead. But after traveling several days, Friar Marcos had yet to see any large cities or any gold. From the natives he learned that

Antonio de Mendoza, the first viceroy of New Spain (Mexico), was a longtime friend of Coronado's who brought him to the New World. In 1539, he sent a scouting party to locate the Seven Cities of Gold ahead of Coronado's expedition.

still farther north was a rich kingdom called Cíbola. And they said that seven cities made up this rich kingdom. Friar Marcos was convinced that these must be the cities described by Cabeza de Vaca. Surely he was close to the Seven Cities of Gold!

THE END OF ESTEBAN

As Marcos followed, Esteban was making his first contact with Hawikuh, the first of the Seven Cities. Hawikuh was a Zuñi town, located in what is now western New Mexico. The slave was overconfident as he approached Hawikuh. Esteban drew attention by wearing "bright robes, tufts of parrot plumage . . . bells and . . . bracelets on his arms and legs." [11] He also carried a so-called magical gourd. Esteban decorated this gourd with two feathers—one white and one red. The "magic" gourd contained small rocks. Whenever he got close to an Indian settlement, Esteban sent messengers ahead with the gourd to tell them of his arrival. With the variety of colors and all the noise of his costume, the slave was something like a "walking musical rainbow." [12] Along the way, he attracted quite a bit of attention, especially from pretty Indian women.

Usually, the costume and gourd impressed the Indians. To show their gratitude and acceptance of the black man, the villages heaped gifts upon him. Esteban received turquoise, animal skins and many other gifts from Indians as he traveled. All of that changed when he arrived at Hawikuh.

Esteban sent his gourd into the town, called a pueblo. His messengers told the Indians that a black man was coming, bringing greetings from white men. The Zuñi did not believe Esteban. They believed it was nonsense for a black man to say white men sent him. The tribal leader angrily threw down the gourd and sent the messengers back to Esteban, telling him to stay away. The slave did not know it, but an enemy tribe used red and white as symbols to identify its friends. When the Zuñi saw the red and white feathers, they thought the gourd was from their enemies.

Esteban was not discouraged, however. Ignoring the warning, he boldly went to Hawikuh. The Indians would not even allow him to enter the pueblo's walls. Instead, they placed him and his companions in a large building outside the town. The Zuñi seized all of their goods and left them

(continued on page 50)

Priests as Explorers

Spanish missionaries like Friar Marcos played a key role in the exploration and settlement of the Americas. In the early years, each conquering force included at least one Roman Catholic priest who acted as a missionary. Sometimes priests served as the leader of a small scouting party, like Friar Marcos. Other expeditions, like Coronado's, included several priests. These priests provided spiritual guidance for the conquistadors and their armies.

The Spanish missionaries went with the conquering armies to convert the natives to Christianity. Wherever they went, Catholic missionaries set up missions. These missions were small communities where the missionaries and their workers offered food, clothing, shelter, and religious teachings to Indians. The Indians also learned new farming techniques and valuable information about raising livestock at the missions. Sometimes, Spanish authorities then used obedience to Roman Catholicism to control local populations. But the Spanish missions offered some protection for Indians who otherwise faced cruelty and inconsiderate behavior from the Spanish.

Besides his first guide, Friar Marcos, four other Catholic priests also accompanied Coronado in his quest to discover the Seven Cities of Gold. Two of them were Luis de Escalona and Juan de Padilla. When Coronado and his army returned to Mexico in 1542, the priests faithfully decided to stay and teach the Indians in "the newly discovered land."* Father Padilla decided to remain in Quivira to minister to the Indians there. A Portuguese soldier named Andrés do Campo and a few Mexican Indians stayed with him. Friar Escalona stayed in the territory of Cicuye.

In many respects, they were "the true heroes of Coronado's expedition, for theirs was the unselfish devotion which gave no thought to gold and silver, but only to the betterment of others."** Both priests were destined to become martyrs for their beliefs. The Indians they loved so much eventually killed Padilla and Escalona.

* George P. Hammond, *Coronado's Seven Cities* (Albuquerque, NM: United States Coronado Exposition Commission, 1940), 69.

** Ibid., 70.

(continued from page 47)

there overnight, with no food or water. In the morning, Esteban decided it was time for the Indians to meet with him. He left the building, but the Zuñi attacked him with bows and arrows. The Indians killed Esteban and many of the others during the attack. A few managed to escape. They retraced their steps and met up with Friar Marcos. They warned him of the dangers ahead.

CÍBOLA

Friar Marcos now faced a difficult decision. His orders were to verify personally the existence of the Seven Cities and report back to Mendoza and Coronado. But the Zuñi Indians obviously did not care for outsiders. Unable to decide what to do, the priest continued making his way toward Hawikuh. Along the way, he considered carefully what he should do. As he got closer and closer to Hawikuh, the reality of the danger set in. Fear finally overcame him and he looked at the city, but only from a distance. Climbing a hill to see Hawikuh, he later described the city as shining like silver and gold. Friar Marcos then quickly left for New Spain. Lacking many supplies, he claimed that he returned

The scouting party, led by Friar Marcos, likely traveled through the Sonoran Desert of Mexico, shown here, before reaching the pueblo of Hawikuh in western New Mexico. There, the group ran into trouble.

south "with far more fear than food."[13] The priest carried word of a great and shining city. He was certain the city he saw was Cíbola.

After the priest reached Mexico, rumors spread quickly. As they spread, they became more lavish and wild. Hawikuh was the largest city in the world. Gold was so plentiful there that the residents made their homes out of it. Soon, any man in Mexico who could go wanted to see for himself if this rich city existed. If it did, great riches certainly awaited anyone who could get there.

But the stories were only stories. Like the stories the Spaniards brought with them to the New World, the tales of the Seven Cities of Gold were too good to be true. Friar Marcos continued to tell his version of the city he saw. Maybe the sun was in his eyes. Maybe the many stories of vast wealth affected his eyesight. Or perhaps he saw what he wanted to see. Whatever the case, the pueblo Friar Marcos described and the pueblo Coronado later found were very different.

As for Viceroy Mendoza, he listened to the monk and believed him. He decided to continue with his plans to organize a large military expedition to discover and conquer Cíbola. The priest's account only increased the desire to seek out the fabled cities. Mendoza chose the young governor of New

Galicia to lead this important expedition. The viceroy picked Coronado because he was "the person closest to him at court and he considered him clear-minded, able, and of good judgment." [14] Coronado was going north to find the Seven Cities of Gold.

Test Your Knowledge

1 How did the slave Esteban communicate
the findings of his advance search party
to Friar Marcos?
   a. He sent samples of the gold he
      discovered back to the friar.
   b. He sent wooden crosses as symbols
      to indicate the riches he had found.
   c. He sent long letters to Friar Marcos,
      using a messenger.
   d. None of the above.

2 What happened to Esteban at Hawikuh?
   a. The Zuñi tribe there greeted Esteban
      as a god.
   b. The Zuñi gave Esteban a sample of
      their gold to take to Friar Marcos.
   c. The Zuñi believed Esteban was an
      enemy and killed him.
   d. We don't know.

3 What did Friar Marcos bring back to Viceroy
Mendoza and Coronado?
   a. Only his story of having seen a great shining
      city from a distance
   b. A small fortune in Zuñi gold
   c. The severed head of Esteban
   d. None of the above

4. How did Mendoza receive the news of Friar Marcos's expedition?
   a. He had the friar beheaded for failing to bring back any gold.
   b. He hailed the friar as a hero.
   c. He believed the friar's story enough to send another expedition.
   d. He did not believe the friar and authorized no further expeditions.

5. What function did priests serve in the Spanish exploration and settlement of the Americas?
   a. They provided spiritual guidance to the conquistadors.
   b. They led scouting parties.
   c. They helped introduce Christianity to local Indians.
   d. All of the above.

ANSWERS: 1. b; 2. c; 3. a; 4. c; 5. d

The
Expedition
Begins

PREPARATIONS

Upon his appointment to lead the expedition, Coronado wasted no time in preparing to find the so-called Seven Cities of Gold. Both Coronado and Viceroy Mendoza spent large amounts of money to make sure the expedition had all the necessary supplies.

It was an expedition based on a grand vision. Coronado was to head north and search for riches on land. Meanwhile, two ships commanded by Hernando de Alarcón were to sail along the Pacific coast. These ships carried extra supplies for Coronado and his land force. Mendoza ordered the ships "to sail close to the coast and make contact with Coronado's force wherever possible." [15] For the Spaniards, it "was one of the largest undertakings ever attempted . . . in the New World." [16] A member of the expedition, Pedro de Castañeda, called the group "the most brilliant company ever assembled . . . to go in search of new lands." [17]

Mendoza wanted the expedition to succeed. He contributed to the expedition from his personal resources. The viceroy gave money, supplies, and even some of his own prize horses. He also used his office as viceroy to help coordinate details for the massive undertaking.

Coronado relied upon the wealth of his wife and her family to provide some of the funds. The young leader made his capital city of Compostela in New Galicia the central place for gathering men, food, supplies and horses, as well as arms

As part of Coronado's expedition, Hernando de Alarcón commanded two ships that sailed along the coast. The ships carried extra supplies for the force traveling by land.

and ammunition from Spain. The king of Spain was entitled to receive one-fifth of any riches discovered, but he did not contribute to the expedition. Finally, after several months of frenzied preparation, the force was ready to leave. It was the middle of February 1540.

A GRAND REVIEW

On February 22, 1540, the large force stood ready to leave on its historic journey. It was a Sunday, and the Spaniards attended Mass. During Mass, the priest prayed for blessings on the expedition. Afterward, Coronado and his force prepared themselves for a review or parade. He and his men marched past Mendoza and other public figures from New Spain.

Viceroy Mendoza wanted to keep detailed records of the expedition. So before the group could leave, Mendoza had one of his officials write down information about each European going on the expedition. These records still exist today. The records were something like an expanded roll call. From this roll call, historians know how many Europeans went on the expedition. Also included on this list was the name of each man and the possessions he took with him. Thus, over 460 years later, historians know who participated in Coronado's expedition and what kinds of equipment and supplies they took with them.

The expedition was made up of about 300 Europeans, each armed for possible battle. Two hundred and thirty of them rode horses, and each horseman brought extra horses for the journey. Coronado organized another 62 Europeans into infantry. Others formed an advance party that met up with Coronado sometime later. Altogether, there were 336 European men in Coronado's expedition.

Besides the Europeans, about 800 Indians also went with the expedition. The Indians carried needed supplies. They also performed various duties like cooking and washing for the army. The expedition also brought a great deal of food, but in a unique way—instead of carrying all that food, live animals were taken. This walking food source included sheep, cattle, and pigs. The group of soldiers, Indians, horses, sheep, cattle, and pigs was practically a small traveling town. The group was so large and traveled so slowly that the

Coronado's expedition sets out across the desert. About 300 Europeans and 800 Indians were part of the mission. The force was so large that travel was slow and difficult. So, Coronado and 80 horsemen broke away from the larger group to travel more quickly.

men who walked had no trouble keeping up with those who were riding horses.

The expedition consisted almost entirely of well-educated younger sons of Spanish nobility. Castañeda wrote that he doubted "whether there were ever assembled in the Indies so many noble people in such a small group of three hundred men." [18]

What kinds of things did Coronado and his men take with them on the expedition? The list is almost as varied as the names of the roughly 300 Europeans who traveled the American Southwest in search of the Seven Cities of Gold. Some men brought many

Dealing with Nature's Harshness

Traveling through what is now the American Southwest, Coronado and his men faced many natural dangers and difficulties. During the summer months, the heat was oppressive. As they traveled through barren lands, the men and horses sometimes went without water. And during the winter, the Spaniards dealt with bitter cold. Ultimately, their inability to handle the cold weather led to problems with the Indians they encountered. Disputes over blankets, clothing, and shelter led to armed conflict between the Spaniards and Indians on more than one occasion.

In one instance, an afternoon rainstorm turned into a devastating hailstorm. Castañeda wrote that the hailstones fell "as thick as rain drops, that in places they covered the ground to a depth of" 18 to 27 inches.* Horses scattered as they searched for items, others brought very little. For example, Coronado took 23 horses with him. The general also had four suits of armor. Another member of the expedition, Diego de Mata, had no horse and carried only a sword and a shield.

cover from the pounding hailstones. Many of the horses suffered bruises. But the hail was more than just inconvenient for the Spanish: The hail damaged much of their equipment. "The hail destroyed many tents and dented many" helmets.**
Worse still, after the storm ended, the expedition discovered that "all the pottery and gourds of the army were broken."*** This made daily life more difficult for the men since they used gourds and pottery for storing food and drinking water. The situation was even worse since the local Indians did not grow gourds or use pottery. Coronado and his men had to do without.

* George P. Hammond and Agapito Rey, *Narratives of the Coronado Expedition 1540–1542* (Albuquerque, NM: The University of New Mexico Press, 1940), 238.
** Ibid.
*** Ibid.

THE EXPEDITION LEAVES COMPOSTELA

The party was so large, that it took nearly a day just to review and inventory it. On Monday, February 23, 1540, Coronado's expedition finally left New Galicia. The journey proved to be slow and difficult. The group, with its large size and many animals, moved very slowly northward. The expedition had only traveled about 300 miles by April 1. Coronado was afraid that such a large group was taking too long to travel the rough country. So in April, he decided to break away from the large group with 80 horsemen and a few other soldiers on foot. Then, he gave orders for the rest of the army and baggage train to follow at their own pace.

This advance party passed through country close to the Gulf of California. This was rich and fertile land. But the land farther north became more rugged and barren. The Spaniards traveling through this territory called it *despoblado,* which means desolate wilderness. As the advance party surveyed the countryside, its members found virtually no food there. Coronado and his faster-moving group continued heading north.

Soon, Coronado discovered that Friar Marcos had either lied or was mistaken about the countryside. At the very least, he greatly exaggerated the truth. Marcos had claimed that Chichilticalli was a lively city of several thousand people. Instead, Coronado found that Chichilticalli was nothing more than a single mud hut in need of repair! Worse still, Coronado and his hungry men found that there was no food. Even so, the group pressed on, still hoping to discover untold riches in what is now the Southwest United States.

Test Your Knowledge

1 What did Viceroy Mendoza contribute
to Coronado's expedition?

   a. Horses

   b. Supplies

   c. Money

   d. All of the above

2 The king of Spain was to receive what
share of the expedition's finds?

   a. One-half

   b. One-third

   c. One-fifth

   d. One-sixth

3 What function did the 800 Indians perform
in Coronado's expedition force?

   a. They provided spiritual guidance.

   b. They did the cooking and
       washing, and carried supplies.

   c. They were warriors.

   d. None of the above.

4 How did the members of Coronado's expedition ensure themselves fresh food?

   a. They brought live domestic animals like sheep and cows.

   b. They had a primitive form of refrigeration using blocks of ice.

   c. They had the Indians gather fresh food and game daily.

   d. None of the above.

5 What did Coronado and his advance scouting team learn about the *despoblado*?

   a. That it was actually a land rich in water, game animals, and edible plants

   b. That gold jutted from the rocks at nearly every turn

   c. That the climate was harsh, the land was desolate, and Friar Marcos's claims were exaggerated

   d. None of the above

ANSWERS: 1. d; 2. c; 3. b; 4. a; 5. c

Cíbola

ARRIVAL AT HAWIKUH

Coronado and his men made camp on the evening of July 6, 1540, in what is now western New Mexico. They knew that only one small hill separated them from Hawikuh. They were very close to the first of the Seven Cities of Gold. Coronado and his men thought that the next day would bring great riches as they entered Hawikuh.

The next morning did not begin well for the Spaniards. First, after waking up, they discovered that two Indians were spying on them from nearby. The two ran away, but later many more Indians gathered there. This larger Indian force yelled at the Spaniards. The expedition's men did not know what the Indians shouted, but the shouting frightened them. As they prepared to approach the city, some of the men were so unnerved that they put their saddles on backward.

Finally, the Spaniards climbed the hill. At last, they had their first look at one of the Seven Cities of Gold. They were not prepared for what they saw. Hawikuh was not a city with gold-paved streets and buildings made of gold. Hawikuh was nothing more than a small village in the middle of a barren and rugged land. The so-called golden walls were made of adobe. Adobe was a kind of clay the Indians dried in the sun. From it, they made bricks. Instead of a city of several thousand people, the Spaniards found a town of about 800 Indians. Castañeda described Hawikuh as "a small, rocky pueblo, all crumpled up"—hardly a glimmering city of gold.[19]

Even though Hawikuh was not what they had imagined, Coronado and his men still wanted to enter it—they badly needed food. But the local Indians, called Zuñis, wanted nothing to do with the strangers. Coronado tried to make contact with some of the Indians who came out to meet him. The Zuñis were well armed. Coronado approached the Zuñis and read the *requerimiento* (or requirement) to them. The king of Spain required all Spanish explorers to read the *requerimiento* to American natives. It was a document that demanded all Indians to accept Spanish rule. The document also required the natives to convert to Christianity at once. Coronado fulfilled his duties and issued the *requerimiento*. The Zuñis answered by sending a flurry of arrows at the general and his small delegation.

THE BATTLE OF HAWIKUH

The Indians' reaction put Coronado in a bad situation. Viceroy Mendoza's orders banned him from killing any Indians as he explored the territory. As the arrows flew, the soldiers begged Coronado for

Coronado and his men expected Hawikuh to be a city with buildings and streets of gold. Instead, what they found was a small village with structures made of adobe, like the one above.

permission to attack. He told his men to wait while he figured out how to pacify the Indians. Unfortunately, the Zuñis did not wait for a peaceful solution. Coronado later wrote to the viceroy that "when the Indians saw we did not move, they took greater courage, and grew so bold that they came almost to the heels of our horses to shoot their arrows."[20] The general realized that his small force was now in grave danger. After receiving the blessings of the priests, Coronado gave the order to attack.

Unfortunately for Coronado and his men, the long journey and lack of food left them at a disadvantage. "They were more in need of . . . rest than fighting."[21] The horses were also tired and underfed, making them useless for the fight. The Spaniards advanced anyway, killing several Indians. The Zuñis realized their disadvantages and quickly sought shelter and protection behind their mud walls.

At this point, Coronado again offered to allow the Indians to submit without further bloodshed. Again, the Indians refused. Coronado weighed his options. He could not allow the Zuñis to resist Spanish power in such a visible manner. More important, the Indians had something the expedition badly needed: food. Coronado gave the order, and his men approached and began their assault on the pueblo.

Coronado later wrote his account of the battle to Mendoza. He said, "The crossbowmen soon broke the strings of their crossbows, and the musketeers could accomplish nothing because they had arrived so weak they could scarcely stand on their feet."[22] Although they were outnumbered, Coronado and some of his men attacked the Indians within the pueblo. The Spaniards reached the bottom of the walls. From above, the angry Zuñis bombarded them with rocks and arrows.

The situation was dangerous, especially for Coronado. He was the one who had read the *requerimiento* to the Indians. His armor was the brightest among the Spaniards. An eyewitness described Coronado's armor as "gilded and glittering."[23] He also wore a plumed feather on his helmet. And Coronado was the one who had just asked the Zuñis to surrender. The Zuñis focused much of their defensive attention on the obvious leader of the strange invaders. Rocks thrown from the walls struck him in the head several times. Finally, one struck him with such force that it knocked him onto the ground. As he stood up, another rock thrown from above struck him in the head. This time, the blow knocked him unconscious. Coronado later wrote to Mendoza that "if

The Zuñi Indians resist Coronado's troops. At Hawikuh, Coronado read the *requerimiento*—a document requiring Indians to submit to Spanish rule and accept Christianity. The Indians responded with a flurry of arrows.

I had not been protected by the very good head-piece I wore, I think the outcome would have been bad for me."[24] As it was, Coronado suffered two small wounds on his face, an arrow in his foot, and "many bruises" on his arms and legs.[25]

Two of Coronado's men, Don Garcia López de Cárdeñas and Hernando de Alvarado, risked their lives to save the general. Lying on top of Coronado, they shielded him as the Indians showered rocks and arrows onto them. Facing fierce fighting, some of his men finally carried the general to safety. Others continued the attack. But the Spaniards were outnumbered nearly two to one. The Spaniards then effectively turned their superior weaponry against the Indians. The Zuñis, equipped with just bows and spears, could not stand up to the armor and muskets of the Spaniards. Pressing the attack, the Spaniards made their way up the ladders to the pueblo. Soon, the attackers were fighting inside the walls. Seeing the battle was lost, many Zuñis turned and fled. Coronado's men captured or killed most of the Zuñis. In less than an hour, the battle was over.

ANGER AT MARCOS

After eating and resting over a period of several days, many on the expedition began to voice their complaints against Friar Marcos. After all, Marcos had described the city as larger than Mexico City

(continued on page 78)

More Precious Than Gold

After Coronado regained consciousness, he ordered the rest of his force into Hawikuh. Then he sent small groups of armed soldiers to raid the surrounding villages. They found no gold in Hawikuh or the nearby villages. But the area was rich in food. The Zuñis were farmers. They raised corn, squash, and chickens. The hungry invaders ate from the Zuñis' storehouses.

One food source the Zuñis relied upon was a kind of corn, called maize. Maize was a multi-colored corn with hard kernels. It grew well in the land of the Zuñi—land with hot, dry weather. The Zuñis ground up the corn in order to make flat cakes. Coronado's men called these flat cakes *tortillas*. Coronado wrote to Mendoza that the Zuñis "make the best corn cakes I have ever seen anywhere."*

The Europeans also found turkeys in Hawikuh. Coronado wrote that the "Indians tell me that they do not eat these in any of the seven villages, but that they keep them . . . " only for their feathers. "I do not believe this, because they are very good—better than those in Mexico."**

Food stores were plentiful in Hawikuh. Coronado and his men discovered beans and venison (deer meat). The Indians had many deer and rabbit skins, which indicated they also ate rabbits. Other game included wild goats, bears, and wild boars. To the nearly starved men of the expedition, Hawikuh was a place full of valuable food.

The food in the pueblo was valuable indeed. One soldier said that in Hawikuh they "found something" they "prized more than gold or silver; namely, plentiful maize and beans, turkeys larger than those in New Spain, and salt . . . "*** The long journey to the pueblo changed some views as to what was truly precious, at least for a short time.

* George Parker Winship, *The Journey of Coronado, 1540–1542* (Golden, CO: Fulcrum Publishing, 1990), 183.

** Ibid., 182.

*** Herbert E. Bolton, *Coronado: Knight of Pueblos and Plains* (Albuquerque, NM: The University of New Mexico Press, 1964), 125.

(continued from page 75)

and shining from all the gold. There was no gold, no treasure, no jewels in Hawikuh. The difficulties of the journey caused many to distrust Friar Marcos. The expedition had failed to find any of the lands or cities or treasures that the priest scouted earlier.

Even Coronado became concerned. He feared for the safety of the monk who had exaggerated the appearance of Hawikuh. It seems that Friar Marcos also realized the change in everyone's attitude toward him. He "did not consider it safe to remain . . . seeing that his report had proved false in every respect."[26] "for they had not found the kingdoms he had told about, neither populous cities, nor the riches of gold and precious stones . . . "[27] When Coronado sent a report back to Viceroy Mendoza, the misleading monk went with the messenger to New Spain.

Coronado told Mendoza that the priest and his stories were anything but true. He wrote the viceroy, "I can assure you that in reality he has not told the truth in a single thing that he said, but that everything is the reverse of what he said, except for the name of the city and the large stone houses."[28]

Less than five months after leaving Compostela, Coronado stood as the conqueror of one of the Seven Cities of Gold. Unfortunately for his expedition, the men soon realized that "the Seven Cities are seven little villages."[29]

Test Your Knowledge

1 What is adobe?

a. A kind of sand

b. A food made from cactus

c. A type of clay

d. None of the above

2 What was the *requerimiento*?

a. A document binding conquistadors
to serve the king of Spain

b. A document demanding that all
native people accept Spanish rule

c. A land grant for conquistadors
who served Spain well

d. None of the above

3 Why did the Spaniards hesitate to attack
the Zuñi?

a. Viceroy Mendoza had ordered that
no Indians be killed.

b. Coronado's men hoped to get food
and water from the Indians.

c. Coronado's men were weak from
hunger and thirst.

d. All of the above.

4 What kinds of crops and animals did the Zuñi raise?

   a. Broccoli, asparagus, and pigs

   b. Cabbage, carrots, and goats

   c. Corn, squash, and chickens

   d. None of the above

5 Why did it become dangerous for Friar Marcos to remain with the expedition?

   a. The men were angry that Marcos's tales of golden cities were false.

   b. The Zuñi were intent on killing Marcos.

   c. Marcos was suffering with heat exhaustion.

   d. Marcos had been injured fighting the Zuñi.

ANSWERS: 1. c; 2. b; 3. a; 4. c; 5. a

From Conquistador to Explorer

EXPLORING THE SOUTHWEST

Though rich in food, Hawikuh did not offer Coronado and his men much in the way of riches. The general wrote to Mendoza that "it does not appear to me that there is any hope of getting gold or silver, but I trust in God that, if there is any, we shall get our share of it, and it shall not escape us through any lack of diligence . . . "[30] Soon, however, Coronado was interested as much in the land as he was in finding gold and silver. The general decided to investigate the surrounding area with small scouting parties. One of these groups learned from the local Indians that a great river was farther west. Coronado decided to explore the land.

Coronado explained his actions to Mendoza when he wrote, "I have determined to send men throughout all the surrounding region in order to find out whether there is anything."[31] He was committed to seeing this through to the end, willing "to suffer every extremity rather than give up . . . "[32] Although the general still hoped to find gold, the teams of explorers he sent out saw many natural wonders of North America. They became the first Europeans to glimpse the Grand Canyon, California, and the Rio Grande.

SCOUTING PARTIES

Coronado sent out three scouting parties to explore the land and report on all they found. Two parties went west and one went east. All three groups saw incredible sights. All three parties accomplished amazing feats just to explore the land and rejoin Coronado.

Hernando de Alvarado led a group of 20 men to scout in the east. This group encountered friendly Indians in what is now north-central New Mexico. They called this area Tiguex. In September 1540, Alvarado's party came across a large river—so large that they called it the Rio Grande, or the Large River. The river was indeed large: It is the fifth-longest river in North America. Alvarado found Indian villages along the river that were much larger than the pueblos of the Zuñis. He suggested that the place might be a good spot for winter quarters.

Another group headed west to find the great river described by the local Indians. Don Garcia López de Cárdeñas led this scouting party. He was the officer who had saved Coronado's life at the battle of Hawikuh. His party found the great river when they reached the Grand Canyon. The canyon was so large and deep that the men were unable to continue to the river's edge. From the edge of the canyon, the men could see the mighty Colorado River far below. From such a distance, the river

Don Garcia López de Cárdeñas led a scouting group that headed west and reached the Grand Canyon. Cárdeñas and his men were the first Europeans to see the Grand Canyon and that section of the Colorado River.

appeared small and insignificant. After trying to enter the canyon for three days, Cárdeñas sent two men into the canyon by themselves while the others waited on top. The scouting party watched the two descend into the canyon and lost sight of them. Late that afternoon, the two men returned. They confirmed that the canyon was very deep and that the river was indeed a large one. They were unable to reach the Colorado River. "Cárdeñas and his men became the first Europeans to see the Grand Canyon."[33] They were also the first Europeans to see this section of the mighty Colorado River.

Still another scouting party also headed west, but its members went looking for the Pacific Ocean. They hoped to meet up with the ships led by Hernando de Alarcón. Captain Melchior Diaz commanded this party. This party never reached the Pacific, but its men were the first Europeans to enter modern-day California. The scouting party led by Diaz arrived at a point on the Colorado River that borders what is now California. It was here that Diaz discovered a message from Alarcón buried at the base of a tree. From this message, Diaz learned that three Spanish ships had arrived many weeks earlier. Unfortunately, Alarcón and his ships had already left for New Spain by the time Diaz and his men arrived. There would be no extra supplies for Coronado and his men.

Sadly, Diaz died as the result of an odd accident. One of the dogs belonging to the group began chasing some of the sheep. Captain Diaz raced after the dog on a horse. The captain threw a lance at the dog, but missed. The lance stuck in the ground. Diaz was unable to stop or turn the horse in time and the butt of the lance struck him. Diaz was badly injured. The captain died a few days later.

TIGUEX

At Tiguex, Alvarado met an Indian who played an important role in the future of the expedition. The man was a chief. Unlike most Indians, he had a large mustache. The Spaniards called him Bigotes, which is Spanish for "whiskers." Bigotes welcomed the Spanish and treated them kindly. Bigotes helped the group as it traveled through the region. He acted as a guide for Alvarado and his men. As they met other tribes, Bigotes told them to be friendly to the Spaniards.

The Rio Grande flowed through a valley rich in resources. Fresh water was plentiful, game was abundant, and the local Indians seemed to have plenty of food. Alvarado and his men found about

One of Coronado's scouting parties, led by Hernando de Alvarado, came across the Rio Grande in New Mexico. Game and fresh water were plentiful, and Alvarado thought the area would be ideal for the expedition's winter quarters.

80 pueblos in the area. Alvarado realized that the location was a good place to serve as winter quarters. He contacted Coronado and told him of

the Rio Grande valley. Coronado agreed with Alvarado and decided to spend the winter on the Rio Grande. The general ordered the remaining army to follow him and his group to meet up with Alvarado at Tiguex. The pueblo was located north of present-day Albuquerque, New Mexico. Tiguex was the largest Indian village in the area. Thus, it had more supplies like food and blankets. Its relative size made it an easier place for Coronado and his men to wait for spring.

NEW STORIES OF GOLD

Meanwhile, Alvarado decided to travel north to Cicuye and explore some of the surrounding area. He took Bigotes with him. Here, the Spaniards found another Indian who shaped the future of their expedition. The man came from a tribe located farther east. The Spaniards called this Indian the Turk, because, they said, "he looked like one."[34] The Turk served as their guide, leading them east until they crossed the Sangre de Cristo Mountains (located in northern New Mexico and southern Colorado). Then they descended onto the plains of the Texas Panhandle. It was there that

This scene of buffalo, painted by artist George Catlin in 1832–1833, shows the animals being pursued by hunters wearing wolf-skin masks. When Alvarado and his crew went farther east, onto the plains of the Texas Panhandle, they saw buffalo for the first time.

Alvarado and his men first saw strange creatures—American bison, commonly called buffalo. The Spaniards could hardly believe their eyes. They had never seen buffalo before. Nor had they seen so many wild animals all massed together in one place. One of the men struggled to describe the great herds he saw: "There are such quantities of them that I do not know what to compare them with, unless it be with the fish of the sea."[35]

As the Turk led the scouting party through the buffalo herds and wide-open plains, he told them stories of a rich land to the east. In this place, "gold and silver were as common as prairie dust."[36] The Turk called this place of such wealth Quivira. Captain Alvarado and his party hurried to rejoin Coronado at the winter quarters in the Rio Grande valley. They could hardly wait to tell the general that their quest for gold was not over—they simply needed to head east, east to Quivira.

The Turk told many interesting and far-fetched tales to the Spaniards. He described a large river that contained fish as large as horses. The local Indians built boats so large there that they required "more than twenty rowers on each side."[37] These great ships were equipped with sails. An eagle made of gold decorated the ships' prows. In addition, the ruler of Quivira enjoyed afternoon naps under a great tree. The tree held many golden bells.

The Turk continued to amaze the Spaniards with stories of great wealth. He claimed that gold was so plentiful that ordinary people ate and drank from plates and cups made of gold. The land was so rich that the people lived in large stone houses. The Spaniards believed the Turk. Maybe they believed him because they wanted to believe that a land of abundant gold existed. Perhaps they misunderstood the man who communicated only through signs. But the Turk did seem to know all

Buffalo

Historians believe that Hernando de Alvarado and his scouting party became the first Europeans to see American bison—animals that are commonly called buffalo. Since they had never before seen such creatures, they described them in terms they understood, as some sort of cattle. The males they called bulls. The females they called cows.

One member of the expedition offered a detailed description of these buffalo. He wrote that "their faces are short and narrow between the eyes. . . . Their eyes bulge on the sides. . . . They are bearded like very large he-goats."*

"They have very long beards, like goats, and when they are running they throw their heads about gold. The Spaniards tested him by showing him some of their jewelry. The Turk easily picked out those pieces that were made of gold and silver. "He knew gold and silver very well and did not care about other metals." [38]

All of this talk of gold led Coronado and Alvarado to make some poor decisions. These decisions hurt the expedition's relations with the

back with the beard dragging on the ground. There is a sort of girdle round the middle of the body. The hair is woolly, like a sheep's, very fine and in front of the girdle the hair is very long and rough like a lion's. They have a great hump, like a camel's. The horns are short and thick, so that they are not seen much above the hair. . . . They have a short tail, with a bunch of hair at the end."**

* George P. Hammond and Agapito Rey, *Narratives of the Coronado Expedition 1540–1542* (Albuquerque, NM: The University of New Mexico Press, 1940), 279.

** Frederick W. Hodge and Theodore H. Lewis, *Spanish Explorers in the Southern United States: 1528–1543* (Austin, TX: The Texas State Historical Association, 1984), 383.

local Indians. And they based their decisions upon what the Turk told them about gold.

Alvarado was a little suspicious of the Turk. After all, the man did not have any gold. When asked about this inconsistency, the Turk offered an explanation. He claimed that he had worn gold bracelets, but his Indian captors in Cicuye—led by Bigotes—took them from him when he was captured. Coronado ordered Captain Alvarado to return to Cicuye and recover the bracelets. There Alvarado met with Bigotes, asking for the Turk's gold bracelets. Bigotes denied ever seeing any gold on the Turk. The Indian accused the Turk of lying.

By now, Alvarado wanted to find gold. He decided to make Bigotes tell him where he could find the bracelets. First, he acted friendly and asked Bigotes and another leader of the tribe to meet with him in a tent. Then he ordered dogs to attack Bigotes. The Indian did not change his story. Finally, Alvarado placed chains on him. Bigotes's people begged Alvarado to release the men. Alvarado refused. The Indians shot arrows at the Spaniard, "saying that he was a man who had no respect for peace and friendship."[39] Considering the ways Bigotes helped Alvarado earlier, the treatment was indeed unfair and rough. Captain Alvarado ignored the Indians' complaints and took Bigotes and the other leader back to Tiguex. There, Coronado held the men as prisoners for more than six months.

Test Your Knowledge

1 After finding no gold, to what endeavor
   did Coronado turn his attention?
   a. Building a city of his own
   b. Exploring the land and its resources
   c. Extermination of the native people
   d. None of the above

2 Members of Coronado's scouting parties
   became the first Europeans to see
   a. the Grand Canyon.
   b. the Rio Grande.
   c. the Mississippi River.
   d. all of the above.

3 Who was Bigotes?
   a. An Indian chief hostile to the Spaniards
   b. The Indian guide who discovered the
      Rio Grande
   c. An Indian chief who helped the Spaniards
   d. None of the above

4 How did the Indian known as "the Turk"
   describe the lands to the east?
   a. A land of immense wealth and abundant gold
   b. A harsh desert
   c. A great plain with many buffalo
   d. None of the above

5 What became of Bigotes?
a. He was hailed as a hero by the
   Spaniards.
b. He was well paid in the gold that the
   Spaniards found.
c. The Spaniards had him imprisoned
   for six months.
d. None of the above.

ANSWERS: 1. b; 2. a; 3. c; 4. a; 5. c

Fighting
and Failure

CONFLICT

As the weather grew cooler, Coronado and his men prepared to get through the winter at Tiguex. The general had sent López de Cárdenas to Tiguex to start building a camp there. López de Cárdenas treated the local natives rudely. He seized their pueblo, their blankets, and their food. Then he commanded the Indians to leave their own homes.

When Coronado arrived, the situation got worse. He and his men were cold. They went to the surrounding villages and took blankets and clothing from the vulnerable Indians. The Spaniards continued to treat the Indians poorly. The expedition members seemed only to care about their own needs. Conflict seemed certain.

The conflict finally came. One day, one of the Spaniards went to an Indian village and saw a pretty woman. He told an Indian to hold his horse while he went after the woman. The man was the woman's husband. After mistreating her, the Spaniard returned to camp. The husband complained to Coronado. The general listened to the story and asked the Indian to identify the guilty man. The Indian claimed that all white men looked alike to him. But he did recognize the horse. Coronado asked the horse's owner about the accusations. The Spaniard denied them. Coronado did not want to convict one of his men based on the identification of his horse. Coronado dropped the case. He did not know that the matter would not end so quickly.

Early the next morning, the Indians gave out their justice for the previous day's wrongdoing. They sneaked into the Spaniards' corral, killing one of the Indian guards. Then they stole about 30 horses.

Coronado was furious. He ordered López de Cárdeñas to retaliate by attacking the Indian village. The Spaniards quickly overpowered the natives, but many of the warriors hid in an underground room, called a kiva. To force them out, the Spaniards threw burning branches into the kiva. The smoke drove them out, and the Spaniards quickly captured them.

López de Cárdeñas then gave orders to execute the offenders. To carry this out, the Spaniards piled brush around stakes in the ground. Then they tied the Indians to stakes. Finally, using torches, they lit the brush piles. Some tried to escape or fought in vain against the well-armed Spanish. When it was over, 200 Indians were dead. Coronado claimed López de Cárdeñas misunderstood his orders. After the expedition, Coronado was cleared of any wrongdoing in the battle.

To make matters worse, the rest of Coronado's army soon arrived. Since they did not have food, clothing or shelter, the local Indians continued to suffer at the hands of the Spanish. The Spaniards violently took whatever they needed from the Indians. Often, they burned what they did not need. Thus, many of the Indians lost all they had to Coronado's expedition.

To avoid the Spanish, many of the Tiguex Indians fled to a village called Moho, which was near present-day Albuquerque. It was a town with good defensive walls. The Indians hoped to be safe there. They weren't. In January 1541, Coronado and his men came up to Moho. Coronado issued the *requerimiento*. The Indians refused to submit. The Spaniards charged, but they could not scale the walls. A few of Coronado's men were killed.

Coronado then shifted tactics. Instead of mounting a head-on attack, he and his men surrounded the town and waited. Since there was no well inside Moho, Coronado knew the Indians could not stay inside forever. The Indians tried to dig a well for water, but about 30 Indians died when it collapsed. After a winter storm, melted snow supplied the Indians with some water.

By mid-March, the besieged Indians faced a desperate situation. With little food or water, the Indians asked the Spaniards for some relief. Coronado allowed all women and children to leave Moho. Within days, the warriors decided to escape. The Spaniards realized what was happening and killed virtually all the Indians as they tried to escape.

QUIVIRA

Winter at Tiguex was a turning point for the expedition. While the Spaniards waited for the Indians inside the walls to surrender or attempt escape, the Turk continued to talk of riches to the east. The thought of gold and silver in large stone houses increased the desire to discover some great land with untold riches. By the time the siege of Moho ended, the Spaniards again focused on their main mission. They no longer thought of anything but gold.

In the spring, the Spaniards prepared to head east to Quivira. The Turk continued to deceive the Spaniards. He encouraged them to leave their supplies so their horses could bring back all the

Coronado leads his men on the quest to reach Quivira. An Indian who was called the Turk told the Spaniards that Quivira was such a wealthy place, its residents ate off golden plates.

gold found in Quivira. Since the expedition failed to find the Seven Cities of Gold, maybe Quivira held the riches the Spaniards desired.

When spring came, Coronado placed the Turk in chains and headed east to find Quivira. As they went, the Turk continued to describe a land of great wealth. Along the way, other Indians told stories of Quivira. And their stories did not include gold or other riches. Coronado suspected the Turk was lying. Worse still, many Indians claimed the expedition was not taking a direct route to Quivira.

After traveling for over three months, the expedition arrived at Quivira on July 29, 1541. This village was near present-day Wichita, Kansas. It did not take long for Coronado and his men to face reality. Coronado wrote that "the guides had pictured it as having stone houses many stories high."[40] They did not find a single house made of stone. Instead, the houses were made of straw. The Turk also exaggerated the size of the settlements. Coronado complained, "I was told that I could not see it all in two months" but "there are not more than twenty-five towns, with straw houses" in the region.[41]

The Turk had lied about the quality of the houses and the size of the towns. But he also lied about the abundance of gold. The Spaniards found none. Instead, one chief wore a copper plate around his neck. The expedition found no evidence of any precious metals or valuables.

Storm clouds loom over the plains in New Mexico known as El Llano Estacado (The Staked Plains). These plains got their name when the Spaniards, on a seemingly endless march to Quivira, in what is now Kansas, marked their way with stakes to avoid getting lost.

After seeing the grass huts and simple lifestyle of Quivira, Coronado knew the Turk was lying. The general and his officers confronted

(continued on page 108)

The Endless Plains

C oronado and his men encountered many difficulties in their great trek across the American Southwest. Although lack of food and hostile Indians posed threats to the expedition, there was another equal danger: getting lost on the open plains. Finding one's way and maintaining direction were important. It was especially hard since the "grass never failed to become erect after it had been trodden down. . . . It was as fresh and straight as before."* Thus, a large group might leave in the morning, but be unable to find its way back to camp just a few hours later. The flat land amazed the Spaniards, especially after having traveled through the mountains. Pedro de Castañeda described it as "so level and smooth" that when one looked at bison, "the sky could be seen between their legs."**

Castañeda marveled at the lack of impact such a large group made on the endless grasslands. "Who could believe that although 1,000 horses, 500 of our cattle, more than 5,000 rams and sheep, and more than 1,500 persons . . . marched over those plains, they left no more traces when they got through than if no one passed over . . ."*** To mark their own trail, members of the expedition

made piles of bones and cattle dung so those bringing up the rear could follow the scouting party.

Perhaps the most unnerving aspect was that the
landscape all looked alike. The plains were so dis-
orienting that "many of the men who went hunting
got lost and were unable to return to the camp for
two or three days. They wandered from place to
place without knowing how to find their way
back . . . "[†] On another occasion, " . . . a man got
lost. He went out hunting and could not find his
way back because the land is very level." [††] To
find their way back to camp, experienced hunters
waited until nearly sunset to orient themselves and
head in the right direction. Later the Spaniards
began marking their routes by driving stakes into
the ground. Thus the vast plateau became known
as El Llano Estacado, or The Staked Plains.

[*] George Parker Winship, *The Journey of Coronado,
1540–1542* (Golden, CO: Fulcrum Publishing, 1990),
180.

[**] Frederick W. Hodge and Theodore H. Lewis, *Spanish
Explorers in the Southern United States: 1528–1543* (Austin,
TX: The Texas State Historical Association, 1984), 383.

[***] George P. Hammond and Agapito Rey, *Narratives of
the Coronado Expedition 1540-1542* (Albuquerque, NM:
The University of New Mexico Press, 1940), 278–279.

[†] Ibid., 241.

[††] Ibid., 236.

(continued from page 105)

the Turk. The Indian recognized that the Spaniards now knew the truth. He finally admitted to his lies.

Confessing all, the Turk told Coronado his real intentions. He and the Pueblo Indians decided to trick the Spaniards to lead them away from their country. The Turk agreed to help because he wanted to return to Quivira. The Indians hoped the Spaniards would become lost on the Plains. Then, with no supplies to feed themselves, they would die in the open country. Even if they managed to survive the trip, the Indians believed they could defeat a weakened force when they returned to the Rio Grande.

The Turk simply confirmed the worst fears of Coronado and his men. After all the effort and time searching for Cíbola, the Spaniards finally faced the disappointing reality: the Seven Cities of Gold did not exist—at least not in Quivira. And the Spaniards were not pleased with the truth. Punishment came quickly to the Turk. After hearing his true plans, the Spaniards killed him by garroting him. This means that they placed a rope around his neck and slowly strangled him to death.

Coronado and his men remained nearly a month more in Quivira. While there, they scouted the surrounding countryside and villages looking for gold. Finding none, Coronado finally ordered the expedition to return to the Rio Grande for the winter. It was the autumn of 1541.

Test Your Knowledge

1 What started the Indian revolt at Tiguex?

    a. The Spaniards repeatedly seized Indian homes, food, and blankets.

    b. The Spaniards treated the Indians rudely.

    c. A Spanish soldier abused the wife of an Indian.

    d. All of the above.

2 How did Coronado deal with the Indian revolt?

    a. He allowed 500 Indian families to leave the region peacefully.

    b. He retaliated brutally against the Indians.

    c. He tried and convicted one of his own men for abusing an Indian woman.

    d. He ordered his men to stop abusing the Indians.

3 The city of Quivira, described by the Turk, was near what present-day city?

    a. Oklahoma City

    b. Wichita, Kansas

    c. Lincoln, Nebraska

    d. Dallas, Texas

4 Why had the Turk lied to the Spaniards about great wealth at Quivira?

   a. He hoped to lead the Spaniards away from the Indian pueblos.

   b. The Turk wanted to return to Quivira.

   c. The Indians hoped the Spaniards would become lost and die.

   d. All of the above.

5 How did the Spaniards punish the Turk for his lies?

   a. They threw him in irons.

   b. They burned him at the stake.

   c. They strangled him with a garrote.

   d. None of the above.

ANSWERS: 1. d; 2. b; 3. b; 4. d; 5. c

Coronado Returns to New Spain

A SERIOUS INJURY

Coronado and his army again spent the winter at Tiguex. This time, there were no stories of gold to warm the men at night. Nor were there many problems with the Indians. Perhaps the greatest challenge facing the army was preventing boredom.

One day, the men were all relaxing and enjoying some games. Coronado and another man were racing on horseback. As they galloped along, the belt holding Coronado's saddle to his horse broke. Coronado fell into the path of the other rider. The other horse struck Coronado in the head with one of its hooves. Coronado nearly died. He was unconscious for several days. He lay in bed for many weeks. He was never the same again. One of Coronado's men wrote that after the injury the general "showed a mean disposition and plotted the return" to New Spain.[42]

After he regained consciousness, Coronado told his companions that a friend in Salamanca had warned him of such an event. His friend was an astrologer. An astrologer is someone who looks at the stars and interprets future events through them. His friend "had told him that he would find himself in strange lands, that he would become mighty and powerful, and that he was to suffer a fall from which he would be unable to recover."[43] Castañeda records that "this thought of death made him desire to go back to die near his wife and children."[44]

Coronado let some of his trusted officers know that he intended to return to New Spain. The army was tired and wished to go back to Mexico. More than two years had passed since the once-proud force had staged a grand review for the viceroy and other dignitaries in February 1540. On that day, there were some 300 Europeans and several hundred Indians who left Compostela with high hopes of gold and wealth. Now, the expedition was smaller and had nothing to show for all its time, money and effort.

Some of Coronado's men wanted to continue on. They were sure that the Seven Cities of Gold existed. They still hoped to find them. But the leader of the expedition decided that enough was enough. The journey had been long and hard. There were no cites of gold. It was time to go home—time to go back to Mexico and face Viceroy Mendoza. It was time to admit that they had failed to find riches.

FACING FAILURE

Coronado discovered that it was more difficult to lead men back to Mexico than to parts unknown. Many began to question his authority. As they got closer to Mexico City, some deserted. Others simply stopped following him. By the time the

Coronado meets with a native during the expedition. After being injured in an accident that knocked him unconscious for days, Coronado decided to return to New Spain.

general reached the capital city, fewer than 100 men remained with him. The expedition that left with so much hope of riches and wealth returned with little to show for two and a half years of hardship. Coronado faced the viceroy with no gold and without discovering the Seven Cities of Gold. Mendoza was not pleased. When Coronado made his report, Mendoza "did not receive him very graciously."[45]

Things were not going well in Coronado's province of New Galicia. While the expedition was away, Indians in the province rebelled against Spanish authorities. They attacked Guadalajara in an attempt to drive the Spaniards out of the region. In part, the Indians rebelled because so many soldiers and other Spaniards left with Coronado to find the Seven Cities of Gold. The remaining Spanish forces were weak and small. The Indians focus of strength was a mountain village named Mixtón. The Spanish called this uprising the Mixtón War.

An acting governor administered New Galicia while Coronado was gone. The province nearly collapsed under the pressure of the Indian forces. Viceroy Mendoza decided to step in and help maintain control. The Spanish lacked manpower so

Mendoza sent Aztec warriors to fight the Indians. The viceroy even gave these Aztec fighters Spanish horses to use in the war. It is likely that this was the first time that Spanish officials provided horses to native Indians in the New World.

In the end, the Spanish defeated the Indian forces. The fighting was vicious, however, and many Spaniards lost their lives in the war.

Perhaps because of their friendship, Mendoza allowed Coronado to keep his position as governor of New Galicia. But this lasted "only a short time, when the viceroy took it himself," removing Coronado in 1544.[46] Later, Mendoza appointed a court (audiencia) to govern the province. According to Castañeda, Coronado's "reputation was gone from this time on."[47]

Also in 1544, Coronado returned to Mexico City. There, he resumed his place as a member of the city council. He still held the seat he first held in 1538. But Coronado's worries were not over. Soon, he faced an investigation of his time as governor and as captain-general of the expedition. This investigation led to charges that Coronado abused his power.

CORONADO ON TRIAL

In 1544, Spanish authorities organized a court to evaluate Coronado's performance as governor of New Galicia and as general of the expedition. All Spanish officials holding an important office were investigated after their time of service. The Spanish did this to make sure their officials behaved while they held power. For 40 days, anyone with a complaint was allowed to appear before the court. Some accused Coronado of failing to pay debts or other financial payments owed to them. Many of these people believed he had taken advantage of them while he was governor of New Galicia. The court heard various complaints from many people. Then the court charged Coronado with failing to pay a variety of debts. After hearing the evidence, the court ruled against Coronado and ordered him to pay his debts. He faced no other punishment, like imprisonment, for these past debts.

Coronado also faced charges made by his enemies. Many were upset with him for failing to find the Seven Cities of Gold. His enemies made many accusations against him. The court officially charged Francisco Vásquez de Coronado with three violations as head of the expedition. The charges included: (1) inflicting excessive cruelty on Indians, (2) failing to perform his duties as leader of the expedition, and (3) wasting munitions and supplies. After hearing the evidence, the investigators declared that Coronado "had performed his duties with faithfulness" and acted appropriately.[48] The court found Coronado not guilty in 1545. Unfortunately for the explorer, the trial hurt his deteriorating status and reputation.

Despite these hardships, Coronado continued to serve on the city council in Mexico City. It seems that Mendoza did not hold bad feelings toward his friend. After all, how could Coronado discover something that did not even exist?

Coronado never fully regained his health. Perhaps his astrologer friend's prediction was right: Coronado was only 44 years old when he died in Mexico City on September 22, 1554. At his death, few realized how great his accomplishments were. Many believed he was a failure since he did not find the Seven Cities of Gold. Few seemed to notice his passing.

From 1940 to 1942, the United States government and several states in the Southwest celebrated the 400-year anniversary of Coronado's expedition. Today, many recognize Coronado for the good and the bad that he accomplished. His attitudes and actions toward the Indians served as the example for future Spaniards. Later Spanish explorers and

A Valuable Possession Found and Lost

Pedro de Castañeda was one of the members of the Coronado expedition. Like the others, he was disappointed that they failed to find gold. But in his history of the journey, written some 50 years later, Castañeda seemed to recognize that the expedition had indeed found something of value. Speaking of their journey, he said, "I have always noticed, and it is a fact, that often when we have something valuable in our possession . . . we do not . . . appreciate it in all its worth."* Although the men who traveled with Coronado "did not obtain the riches of which they had been told, they found the means to discover them."** More important, they found "the beginning of a good land to settle in."*** Sadly, most of Coronado's men did not realize at the time that they held such a valuable possession. The lands they explored settlers continued to mistreat the local natives in the great Southwest.

CORONADO'S LEGACY

It seems that Coronado and others in his day never

and claimed for Spain later became American and Mexican territories. Later, many of those same soldiers wished for the land they had turned their backs on. "Their hearts bemoan the fact they lost such an opportune occasion" to settle down and make a comfortable life for themselves.[†]

Today, the lands that Coronado and his men explored include such sights as the Grand Canyon, the Zuñi Pueblos, the Acoma Pueblo, the Rio Grande, and the Colorado River. Like the men of the expedition, those lands and places are a valuable possession for people today.

[*] George P. Hammond and Agapito Rey, *Narratives of the Coronado Expedition 1540–1542* (Albuquerque, NM: The University of New Mexico Press, 1940), 194.

[**] Ibid.

[***] Ibid.

[†] Ibid.

An ancient Indian compound is preserved at the Coronado State Monument in Bernalillo, New Mexico. Because the Seven Cities of Gold were never found, no one in Coronado's day realized the importance of his mission. But his expedition allowed Spain to expand its territory in the New World.

understood the importance of his own expedition. Since he failed to find the Seven Cities of Gold—which never existed—he never received credit for the vast lands he explored. On his journey, Coronado traveled through parts of the Southwestern United States, including Arizona, New Mexico, Texas, Oklahoma, and Kansas. His expedition showed that North America was a vast continent. Coronado and his men became the first Europeans to see the enormous herds of buffalo on the Great Plains. They also glimpsed, and noted for posterity, many natural wonders like the Grand Canyon, the Colorado River, and the Rio Grande.

Perhaps more important to history, his journey allowed Spain to expand its holdings in the New World. Spain maintained an important presence in North America. And the Spanish presence left an imprint that continues its influence even today: their language (Spanish) and their religion (Catholicism) continue to impact Mexico and the United States. There are also several places that remember Coronado by bearing his name: places like Coronado (California), the Coronado Mountains (Arizona), and the Coronado State Monument (New Mexico). These places "are reminders of the impact of his achievement." [49]

Test Your Knowledge

1 How did Coronado receive his critical head injury?

  a. In battle against the Zuñi

  b. Digging a well

  c. In a horseback riding accident

  d. None of the above

2 What happened in New Galicia during Coronado's absence?

  a. It became one of the richest areas in New Spain.

  b. The local Indians took advantage of the lack of Spanish soldiers and mounted a rebellion.

  c. The land became the first democracy in the New World, with power shared by Spaniards and Indians.

  d. None of the above.

3 For what offense was Coronado placed on trial?

  a. Failing as a leader of his expedition

  b. Wasting munitions and supplies

  c. Cruelty to the Indians

  d. All of the above

4 How old was Coronado at the time of his death?

   a. 44

   b. 61

   c. 52

   d. 70

5 Though he found no Seven Cities of Gold, why is Coronado nonetheless remembered as a great explorer?

   a. Because he obeyed orders to the letter

   b. Because he brought other treasures to the Spanish king

   c. Because he was the first European to see so much of the Southwest, opening these lands to Spanish rule

   d. None of the above

ANSWERS: 1. c; 2. b; 3. d; 4. a; 5. c

Around 1000 The legend of seven bishops leaving Spain and establishing seven golden cities begins.

1492 Christopher Columbus, a navigator from the Italian city of Genoa, reaches the West Indies, claiming the islands for Spain.

1510 Francisco Vásquez de Coronado is born in Salamanca, Spain.

1519–1521 Hernándo Cortés, with an army of only 500 men, conquers the Aztec Empire for Spain.

1527 An expedition commanded by Pánfilo de Narváez leaves to explore Florida, arriving the following year. Narváez and his men disappear.

1510 Francisco Vásquez de Coronado is born in Salamanca, Spain.

1538 Viceroy Mendoza appoints Coronado governor of New Galicia.

1540 Mendoza names Coronado leader of a large, well-armed expedition to find Cíbola. Coronado and his men explore parts of present-day Arizona and New Mexico.

1510

1535 Coronado goes to Mexico with Antonio de Mendoza, the viceroy of New Spain.

1537 Coronado marries Beatriz de Estrada.

1535 Coronado goes to Mexico with his friend Antonio de Mendoza, the viceroy of New Spain.

1536 Four survivors of the Narváez expedition arrive in Mexico City. Their story spurs hope that the Seven Cities of Gold exist.

1537 Coronado marries Beatriz de Estrada, a member of an important and wealthy family in New Spain.

1538 Viceroy Mendoza appoints Coronado governor of New Galicia.

1539 Viceroy Mendoza sends Friar Marcos de Niza north to search for the Seven Cities of Gold. Marcos returns, claiming to have seen the fabled cities.

1541 As he heads to Quivira, Coronado travels across parts of present-day Texas, Oklahoma, and Kansas.

1545 Coronado is found not guilty of charges of mishandling the expedition and committing crimes against Indians.

1554

1542 Coronado completes his 6,000-mile journey and returns to Mexico City with no gold.

1554 Coronado dies on September 22 in Mexico City.

1540   Mendoza names Coronado leader of a large, well-armed expedition to find Cíbola. Coronado and his men explore parts of present-day Arizona and New Mexico, discovering many Indian pueblos, but no gold. Exploring parties also see the Colorado River, the Grand Canyon, and buffalo.

1541   As he heads to Quivira, Coronado travels across parts of present-day Texas, Oklahoma, and Kansas.

1542   Coronado completes his 6,000-mile journey and returns to Mexico City with no gold.

1545   A court finds Coronado not guilty after he is tried on charges of mishandling the expedition and committing crimes against the native Indians.

1554   Coronado dies on September 22 in Mexico City.

Chapter 1
The Seven Cities of Gold

1. A. Grove Day, *Coronado's Quest: The Discovery of the Southwestern States* (Berkeley and Los Angeles: University of California Press, 1964), 54.
2. Ibid., 11.

Chapter 2
The Explorer's Early Life

3. http://www.aboutsalamanca.com/salamanca/history.asp
4. Day, *Coronado's Quest,* 21.
5. Ibid., 22.
6. George P. Hammond, *Coronado's Seven Cities* (Albuquerque, NM: United States Coronado Exposition Commission, 1940), 1.

Chapter 3
Coronado's World

7. Alan Lloyd, *The Spanish Centuries* (New York: Doubleday, 1968), 73.
8. Ibid.
9. Samuel Eliot Morison, *The European Discovery of America: The Southern Voyages, A.D. 1492–1616* (New York: Oxford University Press, 1974), 77.
10. Lloyd, *The Spanish Centuries,* 73.

Chapter 4
Friar Marcos

11. Hammond, *Coronado's Seven Cities,* 7.
12. Ibid.
13. Ibid., 8.

14. George P. Hammond and Agapito Rey, *Narratives of the Coronado Expedition 1540–1542* (Albuquerque, NM: The University of New Mexico Press, 1940), 200.

Chapter 5
The Expedition Begins

15. Hammond, *Coronado's Seven Cities,* 10.
16. Ibid.
17. Ibid., 17.
18. Hammond and Rey, *Narratives of the Coronado Expedition,* 200.

Chapter 6
Cíbola

19. Ibid., 208.
20. Herbert E. Bolton, *Coronado: Knight of Pueblos and Plains* (Albuquerque, NM: The University of New Mexico Press, 1964), 121.
21. Ibid., 123.
22. George Parker Winship, *The Journey of Coronado, 1540–1542* (Golden, CO: Fulcrum Publishing, 1990), 180.
23. Hammond and Rey, *Narratives of the Coronado Expedition,* 169.
24. Winship, *The Journey of Coronado,* 180.
25. Hammond and Rey, *Narratives of the Coronado Expedition,* 169.
26. Hammond and Rey, *Narratives of the Coronado Expedition,* 210.
27. Ibid.

28. Winship, *The Journey of Coronado*, 181.

29. Ibid., 170.

Chapter 7
From Conquistador to Explorer

30. Ibid., 177.

31. Ibid., 176.

32. Ibid.

33. Richard E. Bohlander (ed.), *World Explorers and Discoverers* (New York: Da Capo Press, 1998), 134.

34. Frederick W. Hodge and Theodore H. Lewis, *Spanish Explorers in the Southern United States: 1528–1543* (Austin, TX: The Texas State Historical Association, 1984), 313.

35. Hammond, *Coronado's Seven Cities*, 46.

36. Ibid., 47.

37. Hodge and Lewis, *Spanish Explorers in the Southern United States*, 314.

38. Ibid.

39. Ibid., 315.

Chapter 8
Fighting and Failure

40. Hammond, *Coronado's Seven Cities*, 65.

41. Ibid.

Chapter 9
Coronado Returns to New Spain

42. Hammond and Rey, *Narratives of the Coronado Expedition*, 306.

43. Ibid., 266–267.

44. Ibid., 267.

45. Hodge and Lewis, *Spanish Explorers in the Southern United States*, 378.

46. Ibid.

47. Ibid.

48. Hammond, *Coronado's Seven Cities*, 75.

49. Bohlander, *World Explorers and Discoverers*, 135.

Benitez, Fernando (translated by Joan MacLean). *The Century After Cortés.* Chicago: The University of Chicago Press, 1962.

Bohlander, Richard E. (editor). *World Explorers and Discoverers.* New York: Da Capo Press, 1998.

Bolton, Herbert E. *Coronado: Knight of Pueblos and Plains.* Albuquerque, NM: The University of New Mexico Press, 1964.

Day, A. Grove. *Coronado's Quest: The Discovery of the Southwestern States.* Berkeley and Los Angeles: University of California Press, 1964.

Flint, Richard and Shirley Cushing Flint. *The Coronado Expedition to Tierra Nueva: The 1540–1542 Route Across the Southwest.* Niwot, CO: The University of Colorado Press, 1997.

Hammond, George. *Coronado's Seven Cities.* Albuquerque, NM: United States Coronado Exposition Commission, 1940.

Hammond, George P. and Agapito Rey (editors). *Narratives of the Coronado Expedition 1540–1542.* Albuquerque, NM: The University of New Mexico Press, 1940.

Hodge, Frederick W. and Theodore H. Lewis. *Spanish Explorers in the Southern United States: 1528–1543.* Austin, TX: The Texas State Historical Association, 1984.

Hulbert, Winifred. *Latin American Backgrounds.* New York: Friendship Press, 1935.

Lloyd, Alan. *The Spanish Centuries.* New York: Doubleday, 1968.

Meyer, Karl E. *Teotihuacan.* New York: Newsweek, 1973.

Otfinoski, Steven. *Francisco Coronado: In Search of the Seven Cities of Gold.* New York: Benchmark Books, 2003.

Preston, Douglas. *Cities of Gold: A Journey Across the American Southwest in Coronado's Footsteps.* New York: Touchstone, 1992.

Winship, George Parker (editor and translator). *The Journey of Coronado, 1540–1542.* Golden, CO: Fulcrum Publishing, 1990.

Books

Cantor, Carrie Nichols. *Francisco Vásquez de Coronado: The Search for Cities of Gold.* Chanhassen, MN: The Child's World, 2003.

Hossell, Karen Price. *Francisco Coronado.* Chicago: Heinemann Library, 2003.

Marcovitz, Hal. *Francisco Coronado and the Exploration of the American Southwest.* Philadelphia: Chelsea House Publishers, 2000.

Morris, John Miller. *El Llano Estacado: Exploration and Imagination on the High Plains of Texas and New Mexico, 1536–1860.* Austin, TX: The Texas State Historical Society Press, 1997.

Nardo, Don. *Francisco Coronado.* New York: Franklin Watts (a Division of Scholastic Inc.), 2001.

Weisberg, Barbara. *Coronado's Golden Quest.* Austin, TX: Raintree/Steck-Vaughn Publishers, 1993.

Websites

History of Salamanca
http://www.aboutsalamanca.com/salamanca/history.asp

Conquistadors: Legacy of the Conquest
http://www.pbs.org/opb/conquistadors/namerica/adventure3/a1.htm

Francisco Vásquez de Crornado
http://www.pbs.org/weta/thewest/people/a_c/coronado.htm

Dr. Shane Mountjoy is an associate professor of history at York College in York, Nebraska. There he resides with his wife, Vivian, and the two home-school their four daughters. Professor Mountjoy teaches history, geography, and political science courses. He earned an associate of arts degree from York College, a bachelor of arts degree from Lubbock Christian University, a master of arts from the University of Nebraska–Lincoln, and a doctor of philosophy degree from the University of Missouri–Columbia. He has taught since 1990.

William H. Goetzmann is the Jack S. Blanton, Sr. Chair in History and American Studies at the University of Texas, Austin. Dr. Goetzmann was awarded the Joseph Pulitzer and Francis Parkman Prizes for American History, 1967, for *Exploration and Empire: The Explorer and the Scientist in the Winning of the American West*. In 1999, he was elected a member of the American Philosophical Society, founded by Benjamin Franklin in 1743, to honor achievement in the sciences and humanities.